THE ART OF WOODWORKING

ROUTING AND SHAPING

THE ART OF WOODWORKING

ROUTING AND SHAPING

TIME-LIFE BOOKS
ALEXANDRIA, VIRGINIA

ST. REMY PRESS
MONTREAL • NEW YORK

THE ART OF WOODWORKING was produced by
ST. REMY PRESS

PUBLISHER	Kenneth Winchester
PRESIDENT	Pierre Léveillé
Series Editor	Pierre Home-Douglas
Series Art Director	Francine Lemieux
Senior Editors	Marc Cassini (Text)
	Heather Mills (Research)
Art Directors	Normand Boudreault, Luc Germain,
	Solange Laberge
Designers	Jean-Guy Doiron, Michel Giguère
Research Editor	Jim McRae
Picture Editor	Christopher Jackson
Writers	Andrew Jones, Rob Lutes
Contributing Illustrators	Gilles Beauchemin, Rolland Bergera,
	Jean-Pierre Bourgeois, Michel Blais,
	Nicole Chartier, Ronald Durepos,
	Philippe Gauvreau, Gérard Mariscalchi,
	Jacques Perrault, Robert Paquet,
	James Thérien
Administrator	Natalie Watanabe
Production Manager	Michelle Turbide
System Coordinator	Jean-Luc Roy
Photographer	Robert Chartier
Proofreader	Judith Yelon
Indexer	Christine M. Jacobs

Time-Life Books is a division of Time-Life Inc.,
a wholly owned subsidiary of
THE TIME INC. BOOK COMPANY

TIME-LIFE BOOKS

President	John D. Hall
Vice-President	Nancy K. Jones
Editor-in-Chief	Thomas H. Flaherty
Director of Editorial Resources	Elise D. Ritter-Clough
Marketing Director	Regina Hall
Editorial Director	Lee Hassig
Consulting Editor	John R. Sullivan
Production Manager	Marlene Zack

THE CONSULTANTS

Bob Jardinico manages woodworking sales for Colonial Saw Co., a machinery sales and service company based in Kingston, Massachusetts. He also restores antique furniture in his home workshop in Plymouth, Mass.

Giles Miller-Mead taught advanced cabinet-making at Montreal technical schools for more than ten years. A native of New Zealand, he has worked as a restorer of antique furniture.

Joseph Truini is Senior Editor of *Home Mechanix* magazine. A former Shop and Tools Editor of *Popular Mechanics*, he has worked as a cabinetmaker, home improvement contractor and carpenter.

Routing and Shaping
    p. cm.—(The Art of Woodworking)
Includes index.
ISBN 0-8094-9937-1 (trade)
ISBN 0-8094-9938-X (lib)
1. Routers (Tools)
2. Woodwork 3. Shapers
I. Time-Life Books. II. Series
TT203.5.R69   1993
684' .083—dc20   93-18854
                                       CIP

For information about any Time-Life book, please call 1-800-621-7026, or write:
Reader Information
Time-Life Customer Service
P.O. Box C-32068
Richmond, Virginia
23261-2068

CONTENTS

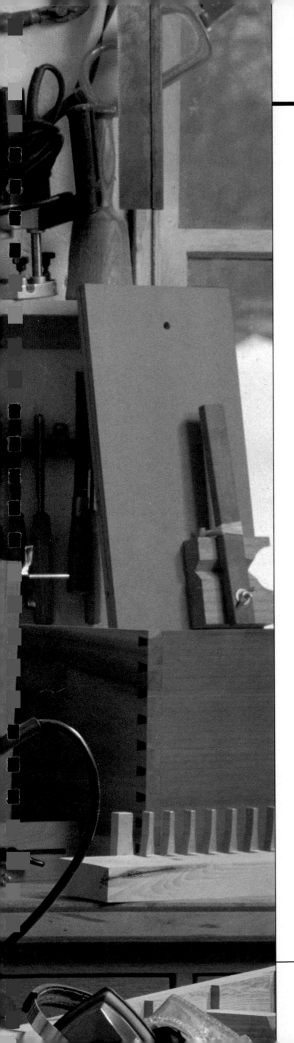

Patrick Spielman on
MAKING ROUTER JIGS

Designing and inventing router jigs and fixtures is somewhat of a passion of mine. Over the years I've made numerous devices—many very crude—to simplify, speed up, or facilitate seemingly impossible routing tasks. These jigs have made my cabinetmaking, relief carving, sign work, and just about every other area of wood cutting much easier and more economical. If you took away my router and my special jigs and fixtures, I would be almost helpless in the workshop.

Jig-making can be easy or complex, simple or refined. The need dictates what you build and how you build it. A few years ago I made a simple but very effective router table and fence with a couple of dollars' worth of material. Just recently, I invested $33 constructing a new router table capable of duplicating the cutting action and operations offered only by a $1500 production routing machine.

Many features of new routers, such as speed choices and easy depth-of-cut controls, can be exploited for better and safer jig-making. Plunging capability is great for some jigs, but for many I still prefer to use the motor unit without the base. Both types can be built into router tables. I've also mounted router motors horizontally on movable sleds with a template follower to make duplicate turnings. You can also mount a router at various angles to the work table. This system allows you to create a variety of profiles from just one bit. For example, a round nose can be used to raise panels and cut European-style finger pull stock for doors and drawers.

Designing jigs gets easier the more often you do it. An idea that inspires one jig will invariably resurface in some form to help solve a different problem. Before building a jig, I visualize the bit making the desired cut. Then I figure out how to attach the router to the jig and move one or the other to make the cut. With more complex jigs, I need to put together one or more mock-ups before constructing the first working model. I make good use of large hose clamps and bandsawn cradles, or V clamping blocks, to hold routers.

I've made scores of jigs to simplify fairly routine woodworking jobs like spacing dadoes, cutting mortises and tenons, making various miters, and scarfing joints; I've even used the plunge router to cut dowel holes. Still, there are a lot of ideas I haven't yet tested, and a lot of jobs that can be made better and easier with just the right jig.

Patrick Spielman, a consultant and author of more than 40 woodworking books, has taught professionally for 27 years. He lives in Fish Creek, Wisconsin.

Joe Truini talks about
ROUTERS

As the son of a carpenter, I learned to respect and appreciate tools at a very early age. I also learned that most tools will last a lifetime, if cared for properly. Many of the tools in my woodshop were handed down to me by my father. There's a low-angle block plane that I use on virtually every project, and a classic DeWalt radial arm saw that will surely outlive me. My favorite acquisition by far, however, is the Stanley 1-horsepower router shown in the photo. My father bought it back in 1959, about 20 years before Stanley sold its power-tool line to Bosch.

This router was already more than 10 years old when I first used it, and although there are newer, more powerful routers in the shop, I instinctively reach for Lord Stanley when I have to shape an edge or mill a joint. It doesn't feature sophisticated electronics, and the collet can be rather stubborn at times, but I've grown accustomed to the way it feels in my hands and to the throaty hum of its thirty-something arbor. Admittedly, old Stanley doesn't perform any better than the newer routers, but it serves as a link to the past: It represents two generations of craftsmen and is a survivor of a once-proud tool line.

It wasn't until my woodworking hobby became a vocation, however, that I truly appreciated a router for what it is: the shop's most versatile power tool. As a cabinetmaker for a custom-design shop in Miami, I relied on the router for everything from cutting simple rabbets and dadoes to milling precise dovetail joints. For the building of plastic-laminate cabinets and counters, routers were used to trim and seam the laminate. I was able to replicate period moldings and fabricate custom paneling right at the job site with the help of a portable shop-built router table. To enhance the router further, I designed and built jigs and fixtures to perform specific tasks. These simple shop-made accessories not only expand the router's capabilities; they also make the tool safer and more accurate.

Now that I earn a living writing about tools, I often report on the latest trends and developments in the world of woodworking. I'm glad to see that routers are more popular now than ever before. Somehow, I'm not a bit surprised.

Joe Truini, Senior Editor of Home Mechanix *magazine, writes about woodworking and home remodeling for do-it-yourselfers. He lives in historic Washington, Connecticut.*

Bill Bivona explains why he owns
A SHAPER

My first experience with woodworking was serving as a boat builder's apprentice as a teenager. I enjoyed working with wood so much that I later enrolled in a furniture building program at Boston University. At both places I found that each of my instructors or mentors had his own favorite tool that could be made to perform many tasks besides the obvious ones. One teacher might use a table saw with an angled fence to cut cove moldings; someone else would fit a radial arm saw with a disk sander or attach cutters to mill profiles. At the school and in the boat shop, the spindle shaper was more often used as a sawhorse or a workbench than as a tool. I was left with the impression that the shaper cuts profiles in the edges of boards and that was about all.

It was not until I opened my own shop that I realized how much more versatile the tool really is. I've had my 3-horsepower tilting arbor shaper for almost 10 years now and I would be lost without it. Woodworkers have personal styles, and I tend to be very machine-oriented. More and more, I find that the hand tools that I once used daily now sit idle in my tool cabinet. For me, end results and speed matter most and I find that the shaper outperforms my old hand tools hands down.

Combined with a decent powerfeed unit, a shaper can cut dadoes better than a table saw and clean up an edge as well as a small jointer. If you have a collet that accepts router bits, you'll quickly find that the shaper outclasses even the largest of routers, with a range of cutters that is unmatched. I recently bought a crown molding cutter for my shaper. It's a stacking system so I can either use the complete assembly to make a cut or install the individual parts to carve separate profiles.

That's only the beginning. Add rub collars and large-diameter bearings and I expand the range of the shaper even more. With these inexpensive accessories I can make a template out of scrap stock and affix it to my good stock. The shaper then acts like a big flush trimmer and I can get perfectly uniform finished pieces every time.

Bill Bivona is co-owner of Hardwood Design Inc. Based in Slocum, Rhode Island, the company specializes in building custom-designed stairways.

ROUTER BASICS

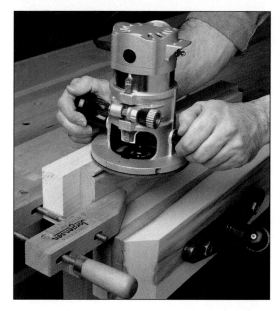

S ince its invention during the First World War, the portable electric router has made its presence felt in every aspect of woodworking. It is easy to see why: The router can cut rabbets, trim laminate, bevel edges, shape molding, and make dovetail joints. It can even surface small pieces of stock and follow a pre-cut template to cut intricate patterns. The sheer number of tasks it performs easily ranks the router with any other portable or stationary woodworking tool. It is as close to a universal tool as woodworking has. The chapter that follows covers the basic principles you need to know to use the tool.

Router motors are commonly available in the ½- to 3-horsepower range. The tool is a direct descendant of the hand-powered molding plane, which featured interchangeable cutters used for grooving, edge forming, and joinery. The router features a motor that spins a bit at very high speed—typically 20,000 to 26,000 revolutions per minute (rpm). Just as the molding plane drew on a range of standard and exotic cutters, the router can use a myriad number of interchangeable bits to create dozens of distinctive profiles, everything from chamfering cutters to beading bits *(page 16)*.

Keeping a router from wobbling as it is fed along the edge of a workpiece to cut a profile into the face can be a tricky operation. A support board clamped to the stock can help keep the tool steady.

Shaping the edge of a workpiece with a decorative profile is probably the task the router is most commonly called upon to perform. There are two ways of making the cut, depending on the type of bit used. A piloted bit features a pilot bearing that rides along the edge of the work, keeping penetration of the cutter constant. With a non-piloted bit, cutting width is controlled by guiding the router along an edge guide clamped to the work.

The manner in which you cut a dado or groove depends on the type of router. A standard tool must be held above the surface of the workpiece before the motor is switched on. The entire tool is then lowered, plunging the bit into the wood. With a plunge router, the base plate can remain flat on the surface as the router is turned on and the bit is lowered into the work.

Any router can be mounted in a specially designed table *(page 29)* that transforms it into a stationary tool, freeing your hands to feed stock into the bit. You can also install bits in a table-mounted router that cannot be used if the tool is handheld. If you have the time you can build your own customized table *(page 32)*; few other accessories are as worthwhile.

A non-piloted bit carves a rabbet in the edge of a board. Riding the router base plate along an edge guide produces a uniform width of cut.

ANATOMY OF A ROUTER

STANDARD ROUTER

On/off switch

Base plate clamp screw
Loosened to set cutting depth or to remove base plate from motor body; tightened to lock plate into position

Depth adjustment ring
Sets cutting depth

Base plate
Supports motor; adjustable for setting cutting depth. Can be removed for changing bits or mounting the tool in a router table, or replaced with plunge base on some models

Handle

PORTER+CABLE

Collet
Accepts shank of router bit; nut directly above collet is turned to tighten or loosen collet

Sub-base
Screwed to base plate; can be removed to attach router to table

Wrenches
Supplied with router for changing bits. One wrench turns collet nut; other holds shaft stationary

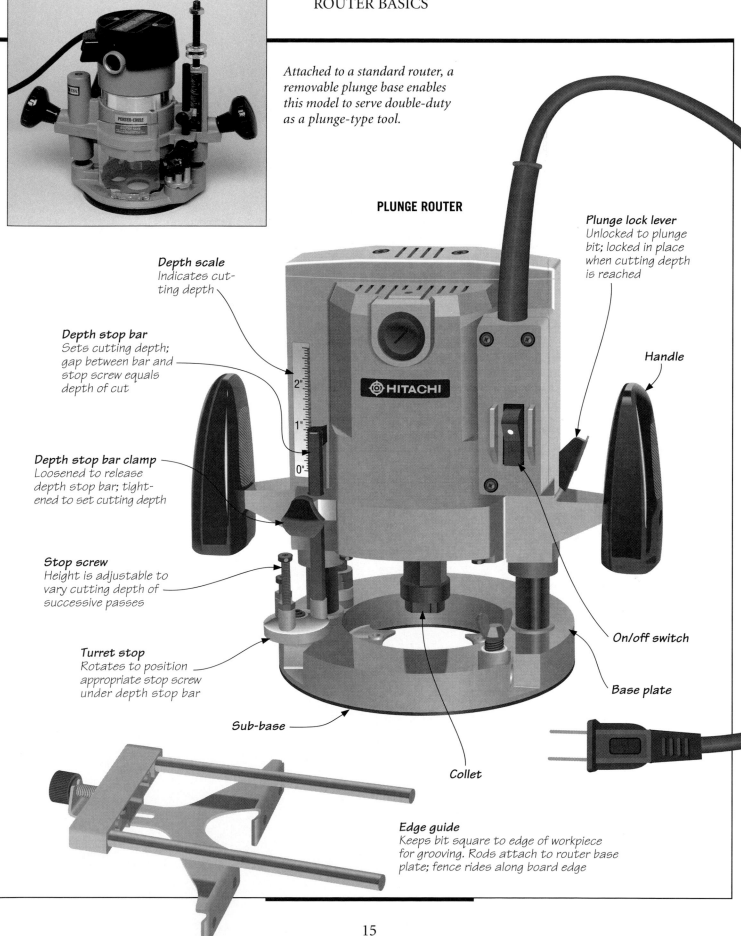

Attached to a standard router, a removable plunge base enables this model to serve double-duty as a plunge-type tool.

PLUNGE ROUTER

Plunge lock lever
Unlocked to plunge bit; locked in place when cutting depth is reached

Handle

Depth scale
Indicates cutting depth

Depth stop bar
Sets cutting depth; gap between bar and stop screw equals depth of cut

Depth stop bar clamp
Loosened to release depth stop bar; tightened to set cutting depth

Stop screw
Height is adjustable to vary cutting depth of successive passes

Turret stop
Rotates to position appropriate stop screw under depth stop bar

On/off switch

Base plate

Sub-base

Collet

Edge guide
Keeps bit square to edge of workpiece for grooving. Rods attach to router base plate; fence rides along board edge

There is a bit for every routing task, from simple grooves to intricate moldings. In fact, there are hundreds of cutters available in a variety of profiles and widths. The pages that follow feature a selection of router bits along with the cuts they make.

A typical router bit consists of a steel body with one or more cutting edges and a shank that fits into the router's collet. Most bits are made from either high-speed steel (HSS) or high-speed steel with carbide cutting edges. Although HSS bits are adequate for cutting softwood, they will not stand up to repeated use in dense hardwood. Carbide-tipped bits, while more expensive and prone to chipping, stay sharp longer and cut more easily through harder wood.

Router bits can be divided into three groups according to their size and function. Edge-forming bits *(page 17)* rout decorative profiles in the edges of a workpiece or cut one or both halves of an interlocking joint. Edge-forming bits generally have a ball-bearing pilot located below the cutter that rides along the edge of the workpiece to guide the bit and precisely control the width of the cut. As their name implies, grooving bits *(page 18)* are designed to cut grooves and dadoes, and work best in a plunge router. The bits shown on page 19 are larger than standard bits and should be used with the router mounted in a router table.

Many router bits are expensive, so store them carefully and use a clean cloth to wipe off pitch, dust, and dirt after each use. Keep the cutting edges sharp and avoid using bits that are dirty, rusted, or damaged.

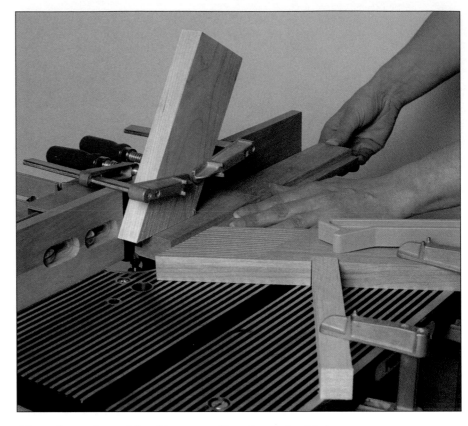

Many decorative molding bits are too big to be used safely in a hand-held router. But with the tool mounted in a router table, these large bits can transform a ½-inch router into a mini-shaper.

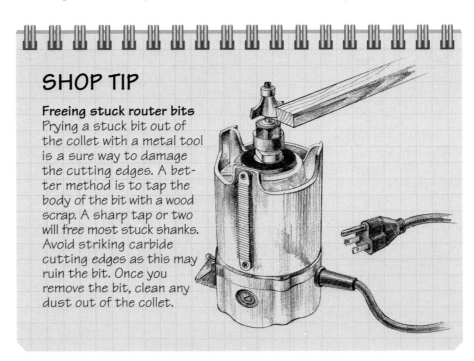

SHOP TIP

Freeing stuck router bits
Prying a stuck bit out of the collet with a metal tool is a sure way to damage the cutting edges. A better method is to tap the body of the bit with a wood scrap. A sharp tap or two will free most stuck shanks. Avoid striking carbide cutting edges as this may ruin the bit. Once you remove the bit, clean any dust out of the collet.

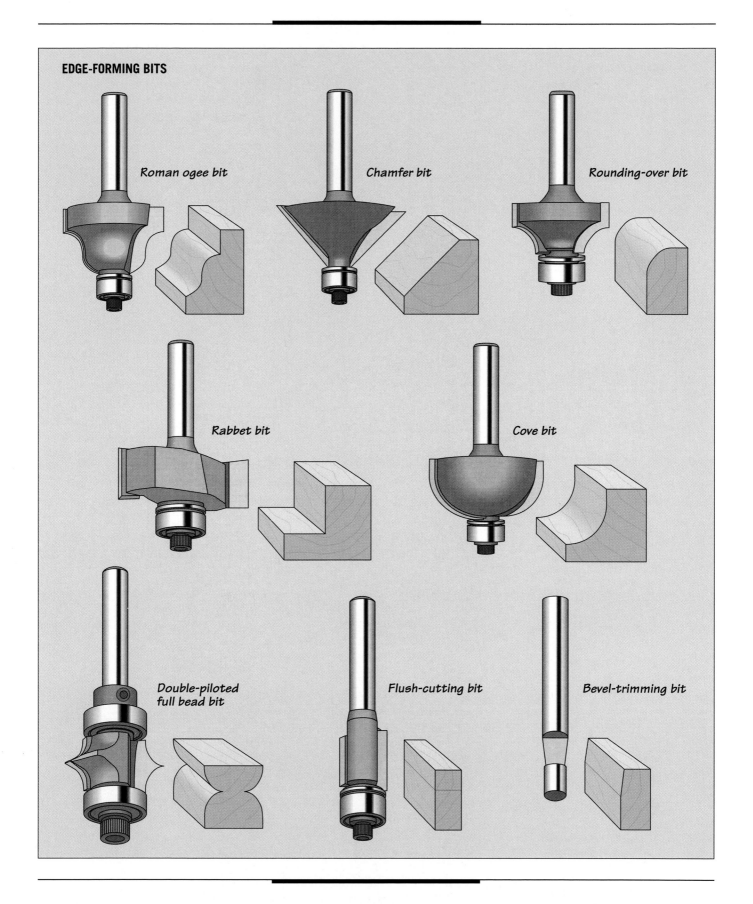

EDGE-FORMING BITS

Roman ogee bit

Chamfer bit

Rounding-over bit

Rabbet bit

Cove bit

Double-piloted
full bead bit

Flush-cutting bit

Bevel-trimming bit

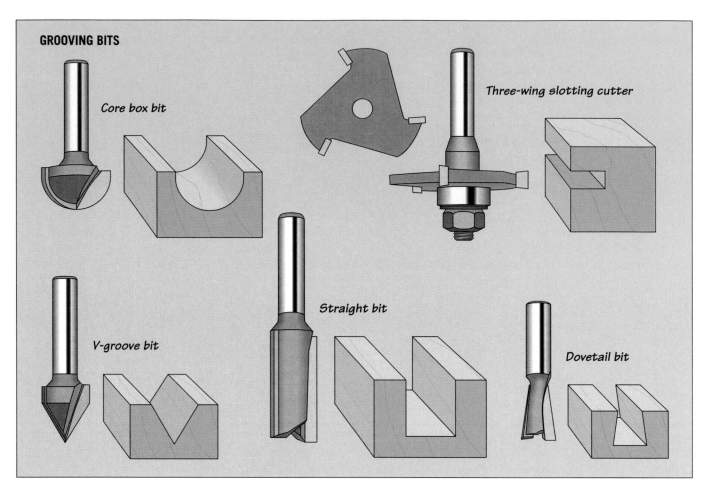

GROOVING BITS

Core box bit

Three-wing slotting cutter

V-groove bit

Straight bit

Dovetail bit

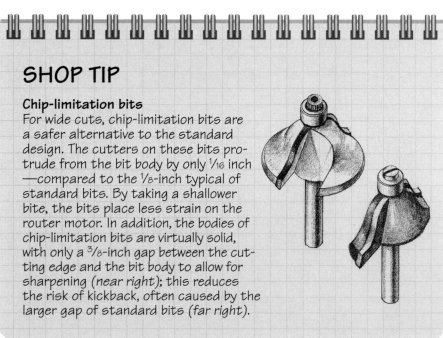

SHOP TIP

Chip-limitation bits

For wide cuts, chip-limitation bits are a safer alternative to the standard design. The cutters on these bits protrude from the bit body by only 1/16 inch —compared to the 1/8-inch typical of standard bits. By taking a shallower bite, the bits place less strain on the router motor. In addition, the bodies of chip-limitation bits are virtually solid, with only a 3/8-inch gap between the cutting edge and the bit body to allow for sharpening (near right); this reduces the risk of kickback, often caused by the larger gap of standard bits (far right).

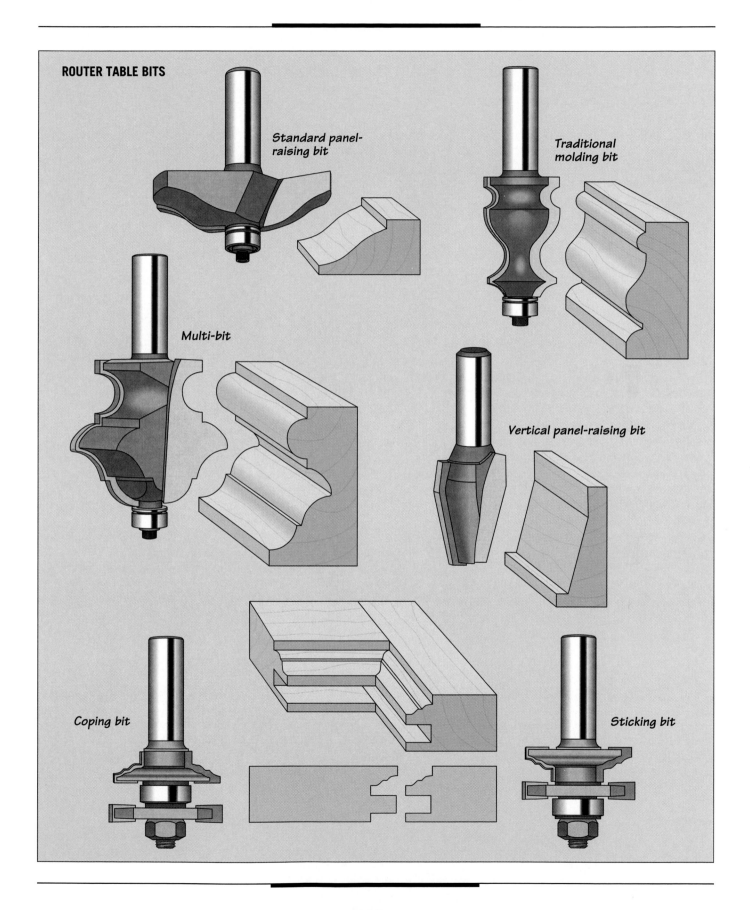

ROUTER TABLE BITS

Standard panel-raising bit

Traditional molding bit

Multi-bit

Vertical panel-raising bit

Coping bit

Sticking bit

ACCESSORIES

The accessories illustrated at right are a sample of some commercial jigs and devices that make the router one of the most versatile tools in the workshop. Some of these products, like the foot switch, make the tool more convenient, especially for models with an On/off switch that cannot be reached while holding the handles. If you use such a device, however, be sure to disconnect it from the tool when you are changing a bit or performing any other maintenance.

Other accessories, such as the vacuum attachment, make the router a cleaner and safer tool. This attachment whisks away the sawdust and chips expelled by the router bit and directs them to your dust collection system.

Other accessories refine the router's cutting capabilities. The circle guide simplifies cutting circles, while template guides allow you to duplicate the profile of a template. A few of the devices on the market are designed to transform the router into another tool altogether. The plate joiner conversion kit gives you the ease and precision of biscuit joinery without the expense of buying a new tool, while the turning jig sets up a router for lathe work. But unlike an actual lathe, which spins the work for handcrafting, this accessory features a manual crank for rotating the workpiece while the spinning router bit shapes the wood.

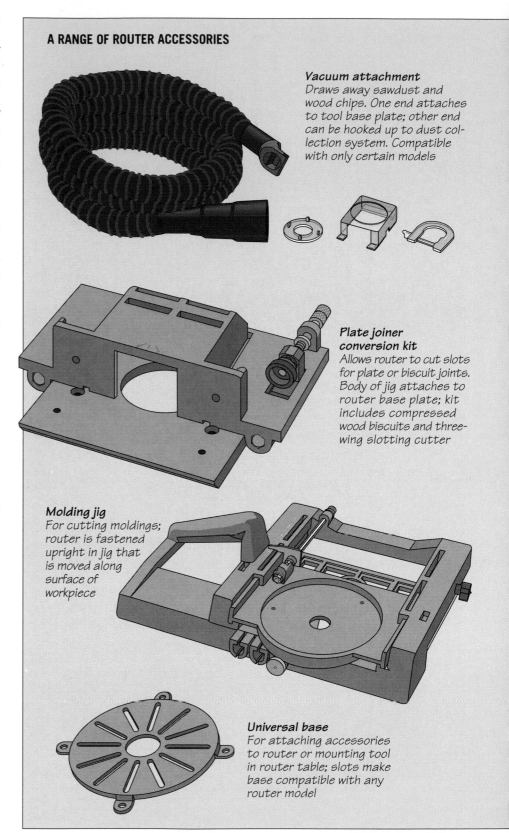

A RANGE OF ROUTER ACCESSORIES

Vacuum attachment
Draws away sawdust and wood chips. One end attaches to tool base plate; other end can be hooked up to dust collection system. Compatible with only certain models

Plate joiner conversion kit
Allows router to cut slots for plate or biscuit joints. Body of jig attaches to router base plate; kit includes compressed wood biscuits and three-wing slotting cutter

Molding jig
For cutting moldings; router is fastened upright in jig that is moved along surface of workpiece

Universal base
For attaching accessories to router or mounting tool in router table; slots make base compatible with any router model

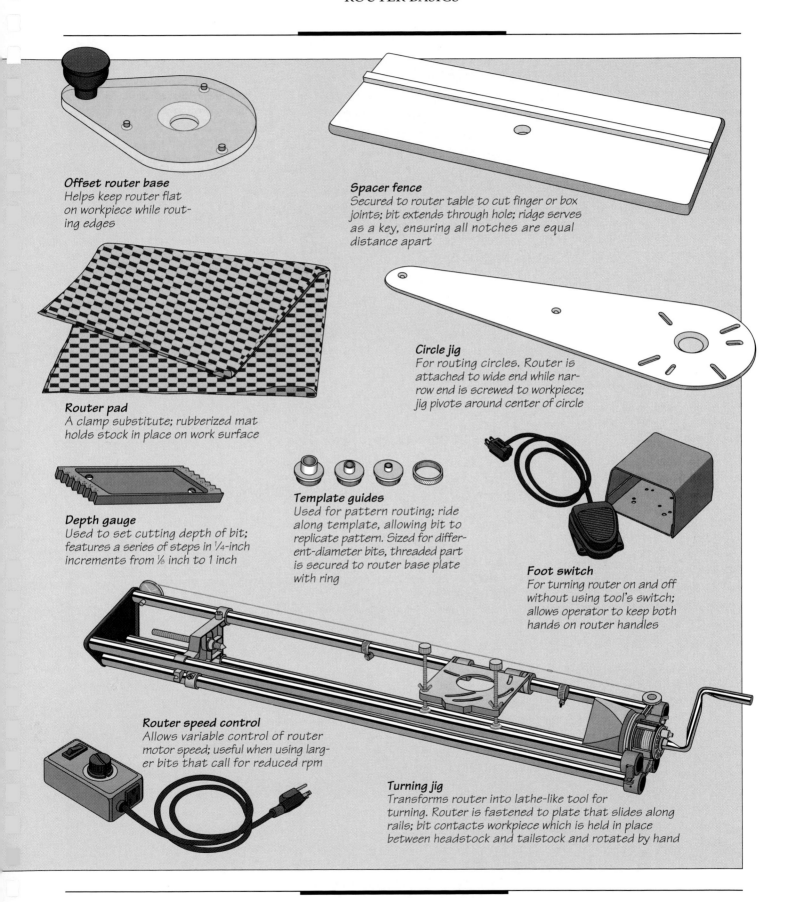

Offset router base
Helps keep router flat
on workpiece while rout-
ing edges

Spacer fence
Secured to router table to cut finger or box
joints; bit extends through hole; ridge serves
as a key, ensuring all notches are equal
distance apart

Router pad
A clamp substitute; rubberized mat
holds stock in place on work surface

Circle jig
For routing circles. Router is
attached to wide end while narrow end is screwed to workpiece;
jig pivots around center of circle

Depth gauge
Used to set cutting depth of bit;
features a series of steps in ¼-inch
increments from ⅛ inch to 1 inch

Template guides
Used for pattern routing; ride
along template, allowing bit to
replicate pattern. Sized for differ-
ent-diameter bits, threaded part
is secured to router base plate
with ring

Foot switch
For turning router on and off
without using tool's switch;
allows operator to keep both
hands on router handles

Router speed control
Allows variable control of router
motor speed; useful when using larger bits that call for reduced rpm

Turning jig
Transforms router into lathe-like tool for
turning. Router is fastened to plate that slides along
rails; bit contacts workpiece which is held in place
between headstock and tailstock and rotated by hand

A router cannot cut with precision unless it is properly set up and maintained. Changing a bit, for example, should be done with care—both to avoid damaging the cutting edges and to ensure that the bit is not sent flying when the tool is turned on. As shown in the photo at right, use the wrenches supplied with the tool to remove and install bits.

If a bit becomes stuck in the collet, gently strike the body of the bit with a wood scrap *(page 16)* or tap the collet with a wrench. Do not try to extract the bit from the collet with pliers; this will damage the cutting edge. Before installing a new bit, clean any sawdust from the collet. Insert the replacement all the way

into the collet, raise it about ¹⁄₁₆ inch, and tighten it in place.

The collet is one router component that may eventually need to be replaced. Periodically check your collet for bit slippage *(page 23)* and runout *(page 24)*, and change it if necessary.

Installing a bit on most routers is a two-wrench operation. With the base plate removed, one wrench holds the shaft steady while the other loosens the collet. Position the wrenches so they can be squeezed together to provide extra leverage.

SETTING THE CUTTING DEPTH

Adjusting a standard router

Set the router on the workpiece. For the model shown, loosen the clamp screw and turn the depth adjustment knob to raise or lower the motor and the bit. Align the tip of the bit with the depth line, then tighten the clamp screw *(right)*. Alternatively, set the router upside down on a work surface, loosen the clamp screw and rotate the depth adjustment knob until the bit protrudes by the proper amount.

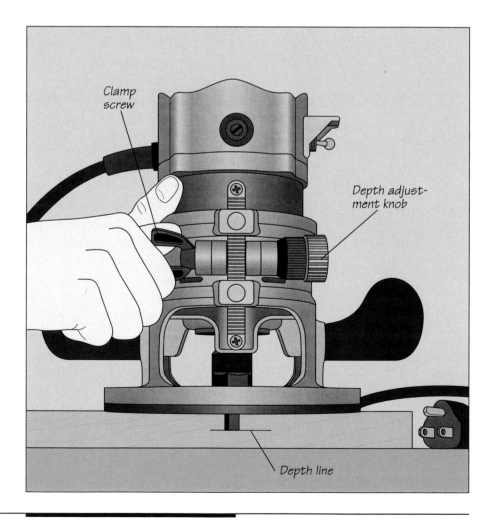

Clamp screw

Depth adjustment knob

Depth line

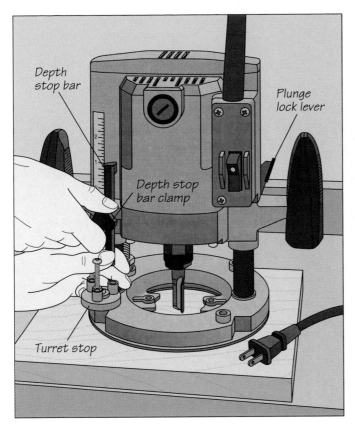

Depth stop bar

Plunge lock lever

Depth stop bar clamp

Turret stop

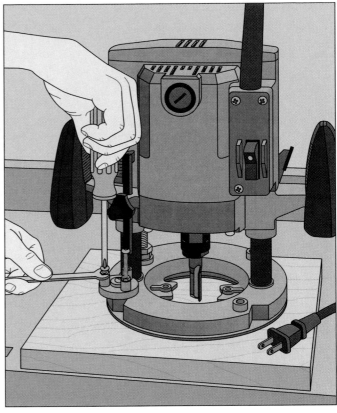

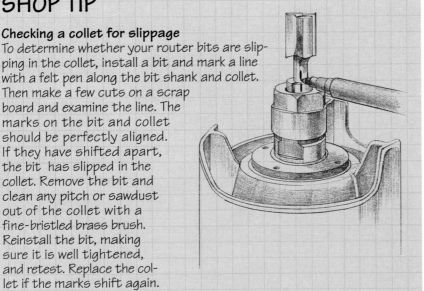

SHOP TIP

Checking a collet for slippage
To determine whether your router bits are slipping in the collet, install a bit and mark a line with a felt pen along the bit shank and collet. Then make a few cuts on a scrap board and examine the line. The marks on the bit and collet should be perfectly aligned. If they have shifted apart, the bit has slipped in the collet. Remove the bit and clean any pitch or sawdust out of the collet with a fine-bristled brass brush. Reinstall the bit, making sure it is well tightened, and retest. Replace the collet if the marks shift again.

Adjusting a plunge router

Set the router on the workpiece and rotate the turret stop on the router base to position the shortest stop screw directly under the depth stop bar. Loosen the depth stop bar clamp to release the bar and seat it on the stop screw. Then loosen the plunge lock lever and push the motor down until the bit contacts the workpiece. Tighten the lever and raise the stop bar until the gap between it and the stop screw equals the depth of cut *(above, left)*. Tighten the depth stop bar clamp and loosen the plunge lock lever, allowing the motor and bit to spring back up. When you plunge the bit into the stock, it will penetrate until the depth stop bar contacts the stop screw. For deep cuts, it is best to reach your final depth in stages. Set the height of the other two stop screws to make passes at intermediate depths by loosening the nut with a wrench and raising or lowering the screw with a screwdriver *(above, right)*.

CHECKING THE COLLET

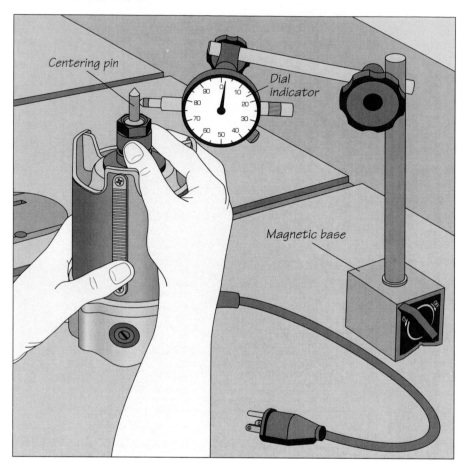

Centering pin

Dial indicator

Magnetic base

Using a dial indicator and magnetic base

Install a centering pin in the router as you would a bit and set the tool upside down on a metal surface, such as a table saw. Connect a dial indicator to a magnetic base and place the base next to the router. Turn on the magnet and position the router so the centering pin contacts the plunger of the dial indicator. Calibrate the dial indicator to zero following the manufacturer's instructions. Then turn the shaft of the router by hand to rotate the center-ing pin *(left)*. The dial indicator will register collet runout—the amount of wobble that the collet is giving the bit. If the runout exceeds 0.005 inch, replace the collet.

Using a feeler gauge

If you do not have a dial indicator, you can test for collet runout with a feeler gauge and a straight wood block. With the centering pin in the collet and the router upside down on a work surface, clamp the block lightly to the tool's sub-base so the piece of wood touches the pin. Turn the router shaft by hand; any runout will cause the centering pin to move the block. Then use a feeler gauge to measure any gap between the pin and the block *(right)*. If the gap exceeds 0.005 inch, replace the collet.

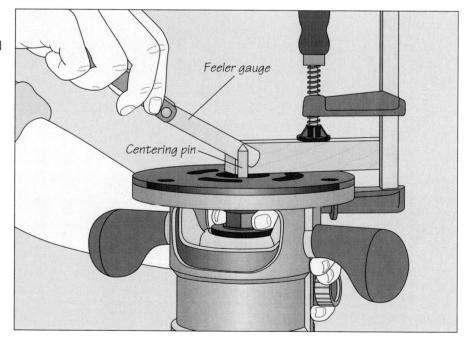

Feeler gauge

Centering pin

Kickback and tearout are two potential hazards of router operation, but the risk of both can be nearly eliminated by using correct technique. With experience, you will develop the confidence and skill that produce consistently superior results.

Always secure your stock to the work surface, using wood pads to protect it from the clamp jaws. This will leave both hands free to guide the router.

Grip the router firmly, pulling it through the work rather than pushing it. Kickback is most likely to occur when you first contact the stock, so be certain of your control at that time. Be especially alert to the danger of kickback when you are using piloted bits with large cutter blades.

When using piloted bits, be certain that you hold the pilot bearing firmly against the workpiece edge at all times. Non-piloted bits demand that you use an edge guide. For a commercial edge-guide accessory, hold the guide firmly against the work as you feed it forward; if you are using a clamped-on edge guide, keep the router pressed against the guide for the length of the cut.

The direction of feed is important in maintaining control of the tool. As a rule, the router should be moved against the direction of the bit's rotation, or from left to right when facing the work's edge *(see illustration at right)*. Apply steady pressure to the tool so the bit is always cutting new wood. If you move too slowly, friction will cause burn marks on the work; too fast, and you will experience damaging tearout.

Be patient as you work, making several small cuts rather than one or two heavy passes. This way, tearout caused by one cut will be repaired by the next.

Here and on the following pages are some tips on safe, sure use of the router.

ROUTER FEED DIRECTION

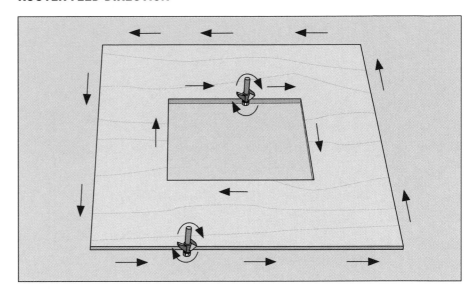

Feeding the router
For most operations, guide the bit into a workpiece against the direction of bit rotation; this will pull the bit into the wood. On an outside edge, move the router in a counterclockwise direction; on an inside edge, feed the tool clockwise *(above)*. Start with cuts that are against the grain so you can eliminate any tearout with the cuts along the grain that follow. Position yourself to pull the router toward you, rather than pushing the tool.

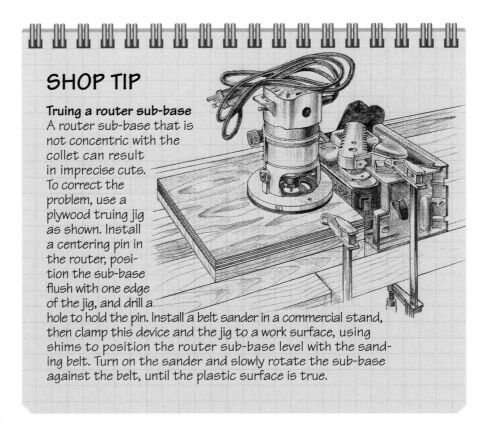

SHOP TIP

Truing a router sub-base
A router sub-base that is not concentric with the collet can result in imprecise cuts. To correct the problem, use a plywood truing jig as shown. Install a centering pin in the router, position the sub-base flush with one edge of the jig, and drill a hole to hold the pin. Install a belt sander in a commercial stand, then clamp this device and the jig to a work surface, using shims to position the router sub-base level with the sanding belt. Turn on the sander and slowly rotate the sub-base against the belt, until the plastic surface is true.

STRAIGHT ROUTING

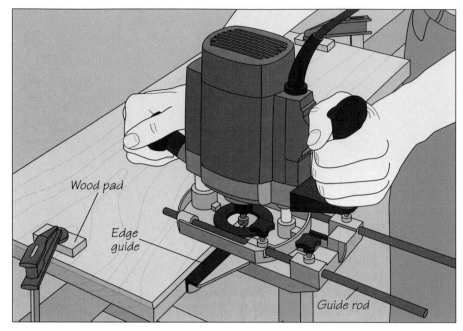

Using a piloted bit
Clamp the stock to a work surface with the edge you wish to shape extending off the table by a few inches. Gripping the router with both hands, rest its base plate on the workpiece at one end with the bit clear of the wood. Turn on the tool and ease the bit into the workpiece until the pilot contacts the edge, keeping the base plate flat on the stock and the pilot flush against the stock *(above)*. For deep cuts, make two or more passes to reach your final depth.

Routing with a non-piloted bit
Install a commercial edge guide on the router, inserting the guide rods into the predrilled holes in the tool's base plate. Adjust the guide so the gap between the bit and the guide fence equals the width of cut. To make the cut, clamp the stock to your work surface. Then, keeping the guide fence flush against the edge to be shaped, start the cut at one end of the workpiece and draw the router along the edge *(above)*.

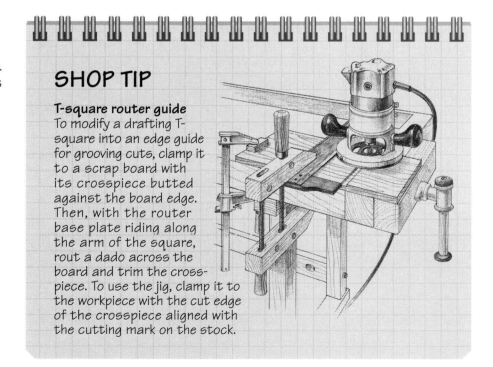

SHOP TIP

T-square router guide
To modify a drafting T-square into an edge guide for grooving cuts, clamp it to a scrap board with its crosspiece butted against the board edge. Then, with the router base plate riding along the arm of the square, rout a dado across the board and trim the crosspiece. To use the jig, clamp it to the workpiece with the cut edge of the crosspiece aligned with the cutting mark on the stock.

A SHOP-MADE SUB-BASE

With its straight edge and large surface, the shop-made sub-base shown at right ensures that your router will remain square to an edge guide clamped to the workpiece while you rout a series of equally spaced dadoes.

Using ¼-inch plywood, cut the sub-base about 10 inches wide and 13 inches long. Taper the sides so the end that rides along the edge guide is wider. Draw a line down the center of the sub-base. Starting near the wide end of the jig, mark a row of points for bit clearance holes; space the points 2 inches apart. Bore a hole at each mark; make sure it is large enough for your largest straight bit. Unscrew the standard sub-base from your router and align its center with each of the bit clearance holes to mark the screw holes in the sub-base. Then bore these holes.

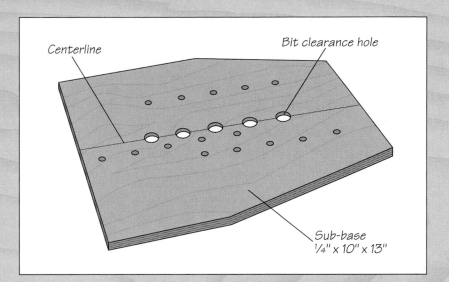

Centerline

Bit clearance hole

Sub-base
¼" x 10" x 13"

To use the jig, screw it to the router base plate so the bit passes through the first hole near the wide end. Align the bit with the cutting mark for the first dado on the workpiece, then butt an edge guide against the sub-base and clamp it in place.

Rout the dado, keeping the sub-base flat on the stock and flush against the edge guide. Unscrew the sub-base from the router and reattach it so the bit protrudes from the appropriate hole and repeat to cut the next dado *(below)*.

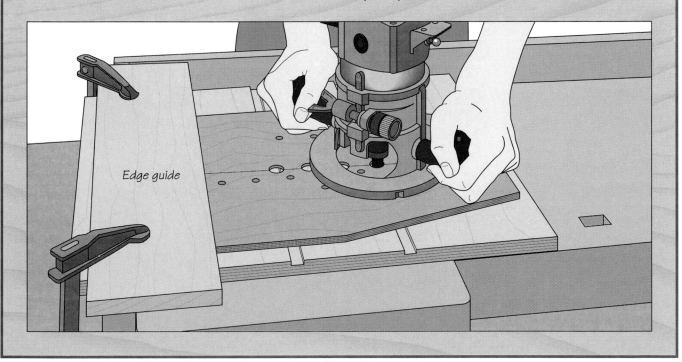

Edge guide

A HINGED EDGE GUIDE

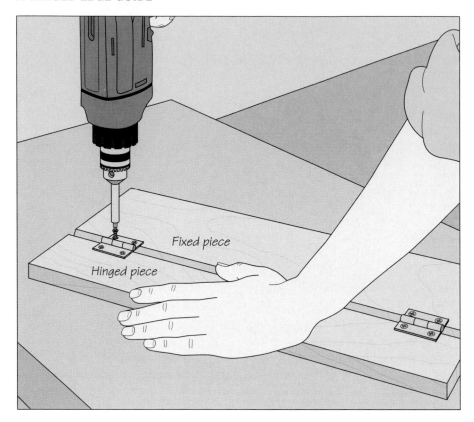

Fixed piece

Hinged piece

1 Making the guide
Although the distance from the center of the router bit to the base-plate edge is constant, remember that the distance from the bit's cutting edge to the base-plate edge will change with the diameter of each bit, and position your cutting lines accordingly. Or, you may want to make several hinged guides, each to be used with a specific bit. Built from ½-inch-thick stock, the guide can be aligned with a cutting mark on a workpiece and simply clamped in place. Cut the fixed part as you would a standard guide, but bevel the top of one edge to allow the hinged piece to pivot. Cut the hinged section so its width equals the distance between the bit's cutting edge and the edge of the router base plate. With their ends aligned and edges butted together, fasten the two pieces of the guide using butt hinges *(left)*.

2 Using the guide
To make a dado cut, set the edge guide on your workpiece and line up the edge of the hinged section with the cutting mark. Clamp the fixed section in place. Then flip up the hinged section and rout the channel, keeping the router base plate flush against the fixed piece *(right)*.

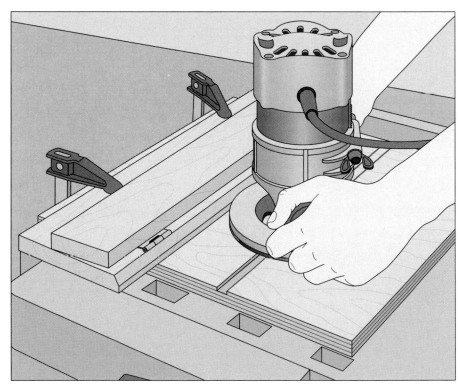

Although your router is a remarkably versatile tool, its usefulness can be extended even further by mounting it in a table. Stationary routing frees your hands to feed stock into the bit, allowing you to exert greater control over the cutting operation. Since a typical router bit spins at 20,000 rpm or faster, this extra margin of safety is a welcome benefit. In addition, some bits should only be used on a table-mounted router. These bits have large cutting heads that exert high forces against the workpiece, requiring an extra measure of control.

A router table allows the router to emulate its larger cousin, the shaper, by making moldings and raising panels—tasks that few woodworkers would attempt with a hand-held tool. In fact, a router table is an excellent substitute for a light-duty shaper, and commercial models are available in many sizes and configurations. Most tables have a guard to cover the bit and an adjustable fence for guiding stock into the cut. If you would like a customized table, you can easily build your own following the designs beginning on page 31.

Cutting depth on a router table depends on how far the bit protrudes above the work surface, while the width of cut is determined by how much of the bit extends beyond the fence. On commercial tables, the fence is usually split. The two halves are normally left in alignment for partial cuts. When you are routing the full edge of a workpiece, however, start with the fences aligned, but then stop the cut a few inches into it. Advance the outfeed fence so it touches the cut portion, then complete the operation. This will prevent making a concave cut—or "snipe"—at the end of the piece.

Mounted upside down in a specially designed table, a router cuts a dado. Attaching a backup board to the miter gauge helps keep the work square to the bit and reduces tearout.

SHOP TIP

A router table on the table saw

To make the most of the space in a small shop, build a router table into your table saw's extension table. Rout a 1/4-inch-deep recess into the top of the extension table and cut a piece of 1/4-inch-thick acrylic plastic to fit into the depression. Drill a hole in the center of the plastic larger than your biggest router bit. With a saber saw, cut a hole in the recess to accommodate your router's base plate. Then remove the base plate from the tool and screw it to the plastic piece. Next screw the plastic into the recess; countersink all the fasteners. Reattach the router to the base plate. A fence for the router table can be cut from plywood and attached to the saw fence when necessary.

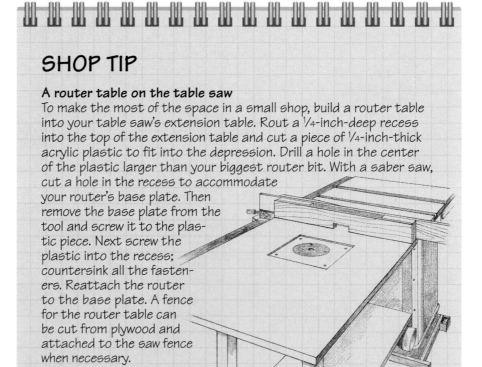

SETTING UP A COMMERCIAL ROUTER TABLE

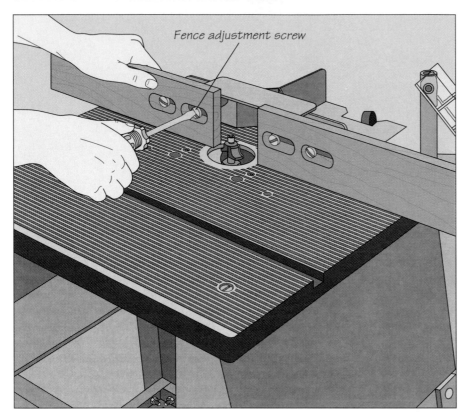

Fence adjustment screw

1 Adjusting the fence
Mount the router in the table. On the model shown, you need to remove the base plate from the tool and fasten the plate underneath the table. The bit is then installed in the router and the tool is reattached to the base plate. To set up the fence for a cut, loosen the four adjustment screws *(left)* and move the two halves of the fence as close as possible to the bit without touching the cutting edges. Tighten the screws, then set the width of cut. Move the fence back from the bit for a wide pass; for a shallower cut, shift the fence closer to the bit. If you are using a piloted bit and want to make a cut equal to the full diameter of the bit, use a straightedge to line up the fence with the outside edge of the pilot bearing, then tighten the adjustment screws.

2 Making a cut
To support a workpiece properly and avoid kickback as you feed stock into the bit, clamp one featherboard to the fence above the cutter, and a second featherboard to the table in line with the bit. Always feed stock into the cutter against the direction of bit rotation. With the workpiece clear of the bit, turn on the router and slowly feed the stock into the cutting edge while holding it flush against the fence *(right)*. To keep your fingers safely away from the bit, finish the pass with a push stick. Position the guard over the bit whenever possible.

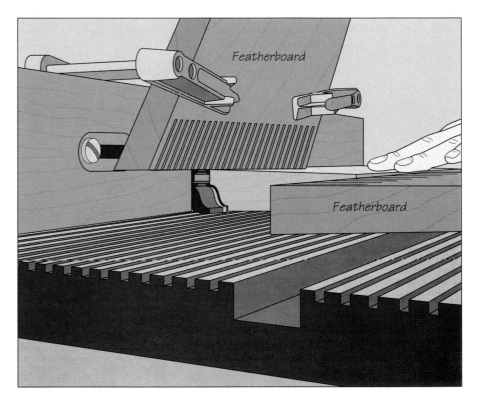

Featherboard

Featherboard

SHOP-MADE ROUTER TABLES

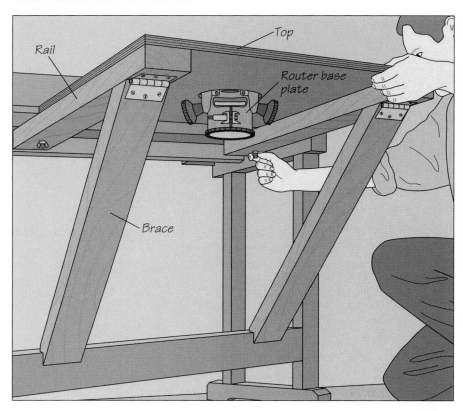

Rail

Top

Router base plate

Brace

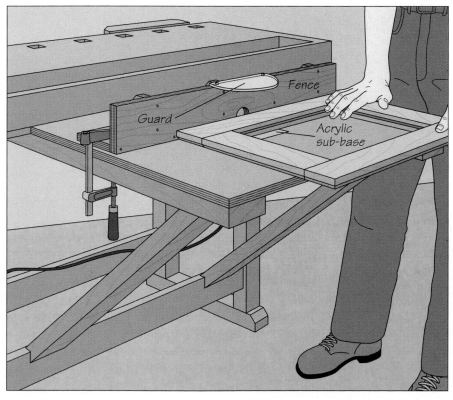

Guard

Fence

Acrylic sub-base

An extension router table

Attached to a workbench, the compact router table shown at left can be easily removed when it is not needed. Size the parts according to your needs. Start by cutting the top from ¾-inch plywood, and the rails and braces from 2-by-4 stock. Saw the rails a few inches longer than the width of the top so they can be fastened to the underside of the work-bench using wing nuts and hanger bolts *(left, above)*. The hinged braces should be long enough to reach from the under-side of the rails to a leg stretcher on the bench. Cut a bevel at the top end of the braces and a right-angled notch at the bottom end. The router is attached to the top with a square sub-base of ¼-inch clear acrylic. Several steps are nec-essary to fit the sub-base to the top and then to the router. First, clamp the sub-base to the center of the top and outline its edges with a pencil. Mark the center of the sub-base and drill a pilot hole through the acrylic and the top. Remove the sub-base and rout out a ¼-inch-deep recess within the outline. Then, using the pilot hole as a center, cut a round hole through the top to accommodate your router's base plate. To prepare the sub-base, drill a hole through its center that is slightly larger than your largest router bit, then fasten the sub-base to the router using machine screws. Set the sub-base in the table recess and attach it with wood screws; countersink all the fasteners. For a fence, cut two pieces of ¾-inch plywood and screw them together in an L shape; add triangular supports as shown on page 33. Saw a notch out of the fence's bottom edge large enough for your largest bit. Attach a clear semi-circular plastic guard with a hinge to allow it to be flipped out of the way. To use the router table, clamp the fence in position and feed the workpiece into the bit, hold-ing it flush against the fence *(left, below)*.

BUILD IT YOURSELF

A SHOP-MADE ROUTER TABLE/CABINET

Built entirely from ¾-inch plywood, the table shown below allows you to use your router as a stationary molding, shaping, and grooving tool. It features a spacious tabletop with a slot for a miter gauge, an adjustable fence, a storage shelf, and cupboards. Start with the basic structure of the table, sizing the bottom, sides, back, shelf, and doors to suit your needs. Fix these parts together, using the joinery method of your choice. The table shown is assembled with biscuit joints. Bore a hole through the back panel to accommodate the router's power cord. For the top, cut two pieces of plywood and use glue and screws to fasten them together; the pieces should be large enough to overhang the sides by 2 or 3 inches. Cut the dividers to fit between the top and the shelf, then fix them in place.

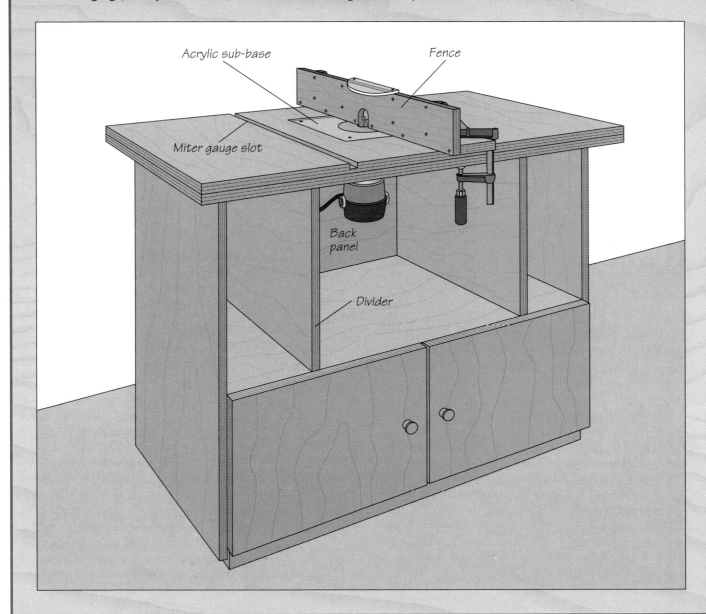

Acrylic sub-base

Fence

Miter gauge slot

Back panel

Divider

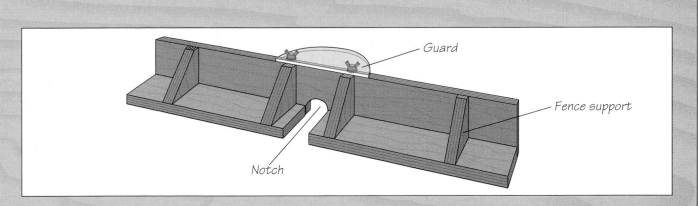

Guard

Fence support

Notch

Use an acrylic sub-base to attach the router to the tabletop as you would for a removable table *(page 31)*. Also, use the same type of L-shaped fence with a guard, a notch for the bit, and four triangular supports screwed to the back for extra stability; the guard on this fence is fixed in place with bolts and wing nuts, rather than a hinge *(above)*. Use the fence to help you rout the miter gauge slot across the top: Clamp the fence square to the front edge of the top and guide the router along it as you plow the slot.

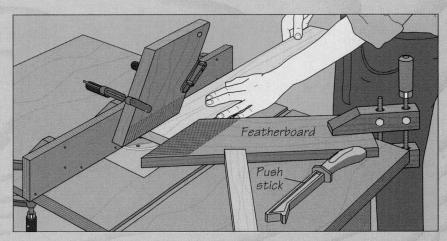

Featherboard

Push stick

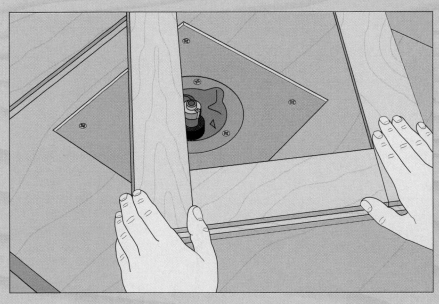

The router table can be used the same way as a commercial model *(page 30)*. For edge-forming operations, set the width of cut by clamping the fence the appropriate distance from the bit *(above)*. Be sure to use featherboards to support your workpiece and a push stick to finish the pass. To make a cut on the inside edges of a cabinet or door frame, remove the fence. Then, holding the frame firmly, butt its inside edge against the bit near one corner and rotate it clockwise to make the cut *(left)*. Keep the frame flat on the table as you feed it into the bit.

THE ROUTER AS SURFACER

A PLUG-TRIMMING JIG

Wood plug

Hardboard
sub-base

Runner

Cutting plugs flush

Equipped with the jig shown above, a router with a straight or mortising bit can make quick work of trimming protruding wood plugs or dowels flush with the surface of a workpiece. To fashion the jig, unscrew the sub-base from your router and use it as a template to cut a slightly larger replacement from ¼-inch hardboard. Bore holes through the new sub-base for the bit and mounting screws. Cut two runners from ¾-inch hardwood and fasten them to the sub-base using glue and nails, then screw the jig to the router base plate. To use the jig, hold it over the workpiece and lower the bit until the tip contacts the surface. Then switch the router on and slide the runners over the workpiece to trim the plugs flush with the surface.

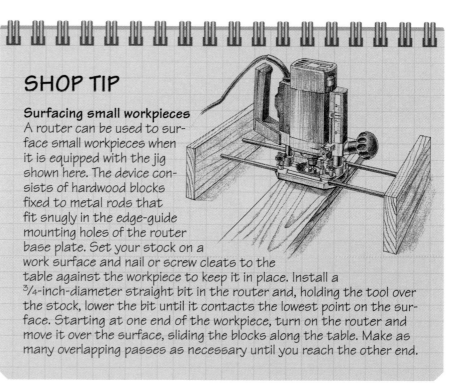

SHOP TIP

Surfacing small workpieces
A router can be used to surface small workpieces when it is equipped with the jig shown here. The device consists of hardwood blocks fixed to metal rods that fit snugly in the edge-guide mounting holes of the router base plate. Set your stock on a work surface and nail or screw cleats to the table against the workpiece to keep it in place. Install a ¾-inch-diameter straight bit in the router and, holding the tool over the stock, lower the bit until it contacts the lowest point on the surface. Starting at one end of the workpiece, turn on the router and move it over the surface, sliding the blocks along the table. Make as many overlapping passes as necessary until you reach the other end.

BUILD IT YOURSELF

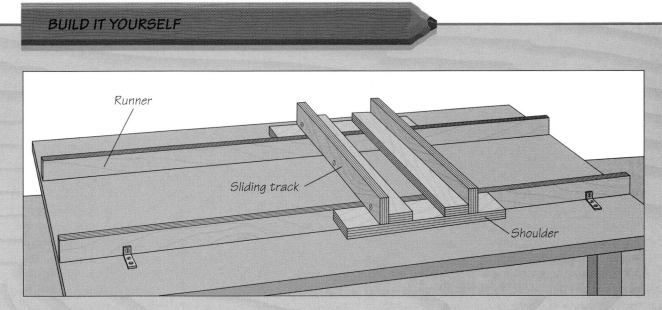

Runner

Sliding track

Shoulder

A SURFACING JIG

Used with the jig shown above, your router becomes a surfacing tool for large pieces of rough stock. Built from ¾-inch plywood, the jig consists of a track for the router that slides along two runners fixed to a work table. Cut the runners 3 inches wide and long enough to span the table. Fasten the runners to the table using angle brackets; make the space between the runners sufficient for the widest stock you will surface. The sliding track consists of six pieces. The four pieces that support the router should be 3 inches wide and long enough to overhang the runners by a few inches on each side. Screw these pieces together in an L shape. Cut the shoulders about 4 inches wide and 12 inches long and screw them to the router supports so the shoulders slide against the outside of the runners; make the sliding track ¾ inch wider than the router base plate.

To use the jig, set the workpiece to be surfaced on the table between the runners and secure it in place with double-sided tape or cleats nailed to the table. Install a ¾-inch-diameter straight bit in the router and seat the tool in the sliding track. Lower the bit until it contacts the lowest point on the surface. Starting at one end of the workpiece, hold the router firmly and turn it on. Slide the tool along one of the vertical supports and back along the other one to make a 1½-inch-wide pass, then advance the sliding track along the runners *(left)*. Make as many passes as necessary at successive depths along the length of the workpiece until it is evenly surfaced.

EDGE FORMING

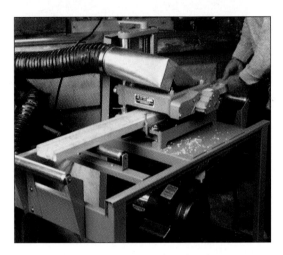

Combining the solidity of a planer with the versatility of a shaper, the molding planer is capable of assembly-line type production of many types of molding, from straight to curved.

The shaped edge of a workpiece often provides the final, finishing touch: a crown molding adorning an armoire top, a crisp bevel on a raised panel, an ogee cut around the edge of a tabletop. These decorative flourishes were once created painstakingly by hand, using planes and spokeshaves; today they are invariably made with an array of electric woodworking tools, chief among them the portable router. This chapter outlines both basic and advanced edge-forming techniques, from pattern routing to making molding.

Stationary power tools such as the jointer and table saw can cut rabbets, and the table saw can also shape decorative edges, but the router is the most versatile, efficient tool for the job. Utilizing a wide range of interchangeable cutters, it can also make cuts that are impossible to perform with any other power tool; imagine forming a decorative bead around the inside of a circular picture frame without a router.

Commercial accessories and shop-made jigs expand the router's ability to shape edges still further. A simple corner-rounding jig *(page 41)* can round tabletops or shelves to your specifications. A flush-trimming guide *(page 43)* helps you trim solid wood edge banding applied to core stock. A veneer trimmer *(page 44)* proves handy for preparing veneer for book-matching.

Mounting the router in a table or pin routing attachment enables you to create more complex edge profiles and elaborate curves. It also provides the stability needed for raising panels *(page 47)*, an edge-forming technique that can also be accomplished on the table saw, radial arm saw, and drill press.

The pin router is perhaps the ultimate shop tool for complex edge-forming tasks *(page 58)*. Essentially an inverted router table, the tool features a pin projecting from the tabletop directly under the bit along which the stock is guided, making the tool ideal for template work. A shop-made pin routing attachment is easily built and adaptable to most commercial router tables *(page 63)*. Remember, too, that not all edge forming must be done with a router. By installing a molding head on the table saw or radial arm saw you can rout detailed moldings *(page 53)*.

Edge-forming bits often have ball-bearing pilots that ride along the stock to maintain uniform cutter depth. Here, a double-fluted beading bit carves a decorative profile around the circumference of a tabletop.

BASIC EDGE SHAPING

Making multiple copies of the same contoured shape with the router requires the use of a straightedge, a jig, or a template to guide the tool along the edge of a workpiece.

With a template, your router can make quick work of repeating a curved cut in a series of workpieces. The exact procedure you follow depends on the type of bit you are using. With the piloted bit shown below, the cutting edge is below the pilot and the template is clamped atop the workpiece. The pilot will follow the curved edge of the template while the cutters reproduce the same curve on the workpiece.

When you use a non-piloted bit, attach a template guide to the router base plate. The guide is a metal collar that surrounds the bit shank and protrudes slightly from the bottom of the

A support board secured alongside a workpiece during an edge-forming operation keeps the router steady. For contour cuts, use the waste piece that remains after sawing the curve.

router's sub-base. With the template secured atop the stock, the guide rides along the edge of the pattern, enabling the bit to shape the workpiece.

Whichever type of bit you use, make the template from durable wood, such as plywood or particleboard. Cut the pattern using a band saw or a saber saw, then carefully sand the edges that will be guiding the router, since any imperfections in the template will be duplicated on the workpiece.

For a non-piloted bit, make the template slightly thicker than the height of the template guide. With a piloted bit, the template should be thick enough to provide an adequate bearing surface for the pilot.

To round the corners of a tabletop or shelf, you can use a shop-made jig like the one shown on page 41.

PATTERN ROUTING WITH A PILOTED BIT

Making the cut
Make a template that is precisely the same size as the finished pieces you wish to cut. Use the template to outline the pattern on your workpiece, then cut out most of the waste with a band saw or saber saw, leaving about $\frac{1}{16}$ inch of stock beyond the cutting line. Use double-sided tape to fasten the workpiece to the template, ensuring that the straight edges of the boards are aligned. Clamp the two pieces to a work surface. Holding the router with both hands, rest its base plate on the template at one end with the bit clear of the wood and turn on the tool. Ease the bit into the stock until the pilot contacts the edge, then pull the router toward the other end of the cut, keeping the base plate flat on the template and the pilot flush against its edge *(right)*.

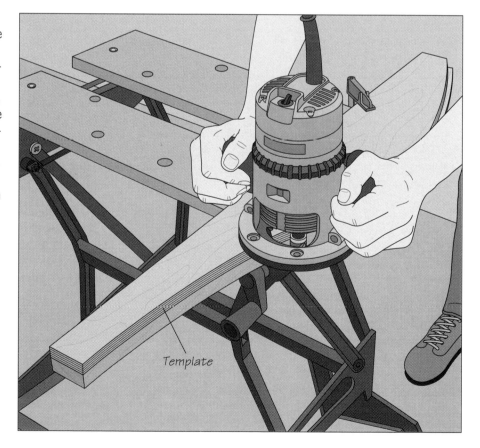

Template

USING A TEMPLATE GUIDE

1 Installing a template guide
Loosen the clamp screw on the router base plate and remove the plate. Insert the threaded part of the template guide through the hole in the middle of the sub-base *(right)*, then screw on the locking ring to hold the two together. The diameter of the template guide should be as close to that of the bit as possible without touching the cutting edges. Reassemble the router.

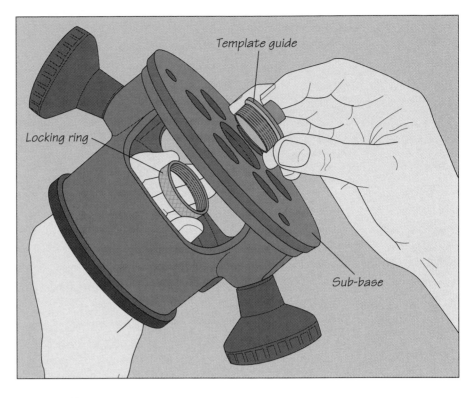

2 Making the cut
Prepare a template that is slightly smaller than the finished piece to compensate for the difference between the bit diameter and the diameter of the template guide. Fasten the template atop the workpiece with double-sided tape, then clamp the two pieces to a work surface. Cut the pattern as you would with a piloted bit, feeding the cutter into the stock until the template guide contacts the template. Complete the cut, making sure that the guide is pressed against the edge of the pattern throughout the operation *(left)*.

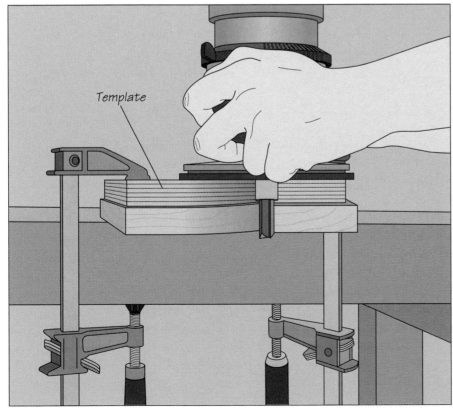

ROUNDING CORNERS

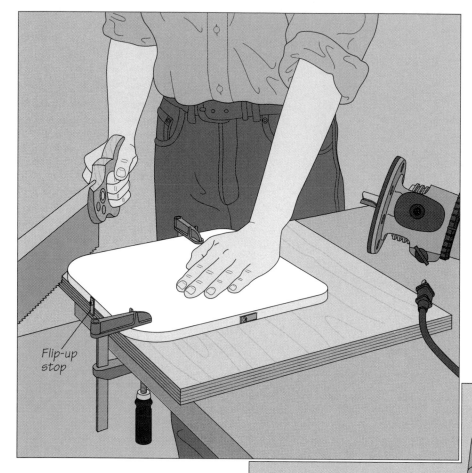

Flip-up stop

1 Sawing the excess waste
You can use a commercial corner-rounding jig to curve the corners of a workpiece. Set your stock on a work surface and place the jig atop the corner to be rounded. Set the flip-up stops on the jig in the vertical position to align the edges of the jig with those of the workpiece. Clamp the two pieces to the work surface. To make the router cut easier, saw away the bulk of the waste *(left)*.

2 Rounding the corner
Using a top-piloted flush-cutting bit, start clear of the corner, making the cut as you would when pattern routing with a piloted bit *(page 38)*. Keep the bit pilot pressed against the edge of the jig throughout the operation *(right)*.

BUILD IT YOURSELF

UNDERSIDE VIEW

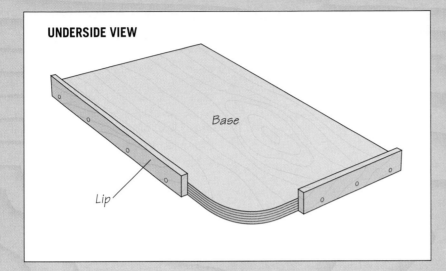

Base

Lip

A CORNER-ROUNDING JIG

Easy and inexpensive to build, the corner-rounding jig at left works as well as the commercial version shown on the previous page. The jig consists of a plywood base and two lips that keep the edges of the jig and the work-piece aligned.

Cut the base from a piece of ³⁄₄-inch plywood. For most jobs, a base about 10 inches wide and 16 inches long will be adequate. Draw the curve you wish to rout on the base near one corner, then make the cut with a band saw or a saber saw; sand the edge smooth. You can also cut the corner using a router attached to a circle-cutting guide *(page 79)*.

Cut the lips from stock ¹⁄₂ inch thick and 1¹⁄₂ inches wide, then nail or screw the pieces to the base, leaving about 3 to 4 inches between each lip and the rounded corner. The top edge of the lips should be flush with the top surface of the base.

To use the jig, set your stock on a work surface with the corner to be rounded extending off the table by several inches. Place the jig on top of the workpiece so the lips are butted against the edges of the stock. Use clamps to secure the two pieces to the work surface. Make the cut as you would with a commercial jig, pressing the bit's pilot against the edge of the jig throughout *(left, bottom)*.

CUTTING AND TRIMMING PLASTIC LAMINATES

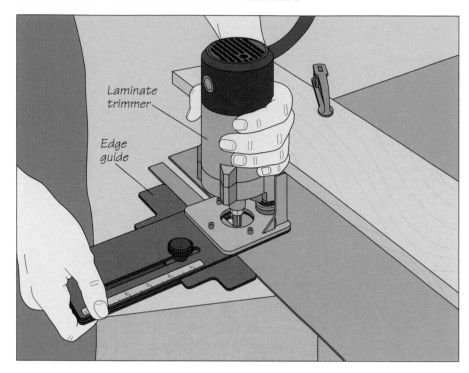

1 Cutting strips of edging
Use a laminate trimmer with a commercial edge guide to cut strips of edging from a sheet of laminate. The guide ensures that the width of each strip is uniform. Attach the guide to the trimmer (on the model shown, the trimmer's sub-base is removed and the edge guide is fastened to the tool's base plate); then adjust the width of cut following the manufacturer's instructions. Install a straight bit in the trimmer and clamp the sheet to a work surface, using a board to keep the sheet flat. With the bit clear of the sheet, start the cut at one end. Holding the trimmer with one hand, feed the tool toward the opposite end; use your other hand to press the guide flush against the edge of the sheet *(left)*.

2 Installing and trimming the laminate
Glue the banding onto the edges of the workpiece and clamp the panel edge-up. Remove the edge guide from the trimmer and install the sub-base and a flush-cutting bit. Use the tool to trim any banding that projects beyond the edges of the workpiece. Repeat to glue and trim edging on the ends of the panel. Glue the top laminate in place next. To trim it flush with the edges, hold the trimmer firmly with one hand and guide the tool along the workpiece *(right)*. To make an interior cut to match a cutout in the panel, clamp the panel to the work surface. Install a pilot panel bit in the trimmer and plunge the bit's sharpened tip into the sheet to pierce it, then feed the trimmer until the pilot contacts the edge of the cutout. Making sure that the pilot remains flush against the edge of the cutout *(inset)*, complete the cut.

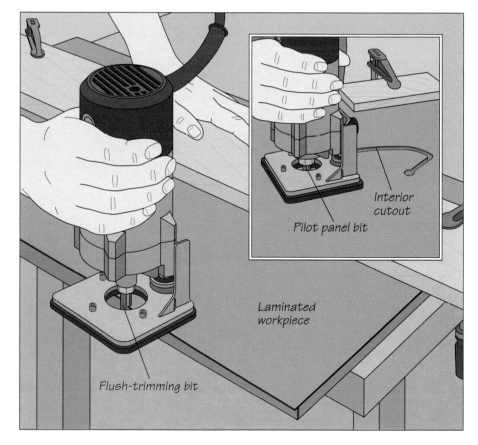

BUILD IT YOURSELF

A FLUSH-TRIMMING JIG

The jig shown at right allows you to use a non-piloted straight bit to trim solid edge banding flush with the top and bottom surfaces of a panel. Designed to be screwed to the tool's sub-base, the jig features two guide pins that ride along the outside face of the banding while the end of the bit trims the banding.

To make the jig, cut the base from ½-inch plywood and the body from ¾-inch plywood. Make the width of both pieces equal to the diameter of your router base plate; cut the body about 12 inches long and the base 8 inches long. Use the tool's sub-base as a template to cut the curve at one end of the jig body. Also cut a 3-inch-diameter hole through the body to clear the bit, but leave a section within the circle to house the guide pins. Cut one end of the jig

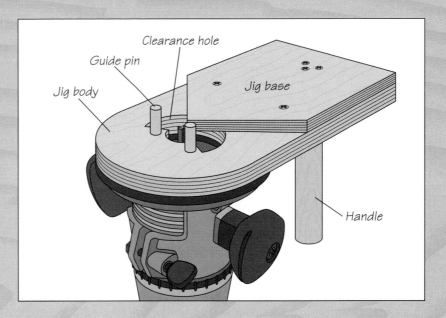

base to a point, then screw the base to the jig body; countersink the fasteners. Bore two ⅝-inch-diameter holes through the wedge in the body

and glue two short lengths of dowels in the holes; position the holes so the bit will line up directly over the edge of the banding with the guide pins flush against the stock. To complete the jig, cut a length of dowel for a handle and screw it to the body.

To use the jig, attach the router's sub-base to the body with screws. Install a straight bit in the tool and adjust the cutting depth so the tip of the bit is level with the bottom of the jig base. Clamp your stock to a work surface, protecting it with a wood pad. With the bit clear of the workpiece, turn on the router and set the jig base on the top of the stock. Butting the guide pins against the outside surface of the banding, guide the router along the top edge, trimming the banding *(left)*. Apply downward pressure on the handle throughout the operation to keep the router from tipping.

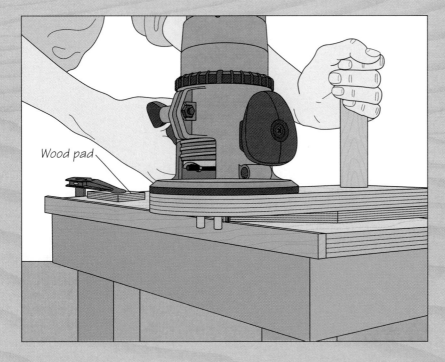

BUILD IT YOURSELF

A VENEER-TRIMMING GUIDE

Trim sheets of veneer to width quickly and accurately on a router table with the jig shown at right. The veneer is sandwiched between the base and top of the jig; the base rides along the pilot of a flush-cutting bit, which cuts the veneer flush with the edge of the jig *(right, middle)*.

Cut the base from 1½-inch-thick stock and the top from ¾-inch-thick stock. Make the pieces about 6 inches wide; the base should be a few inches longer than your router table, and the top long enough to cover the veneer. Choose a board with a slight bow for the top, if possible; with the bow facing down, applying clamping pressure near the ends of the board will flatten it, producing uniform pressure against the base. Screw toggle clamps to the base so the top will fit between them.

To prepare your router table for the operation, install the bit on the router

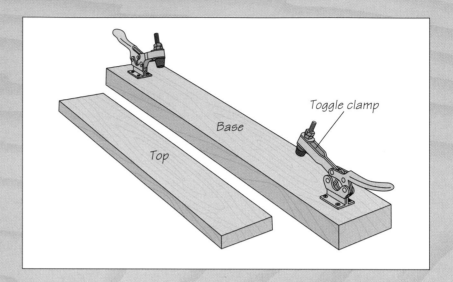

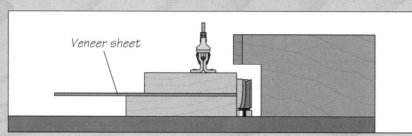

and mount the tool in the table. Cut a guard from a piece of stock, sawing a notch from one edge to form a lip that will cover the cutter. Clamp the guard to the table.

To use the jig, place the veneer to be trimmed between the base and the top so the grain of the veneer is parallel to that of the boards. The edges of the sheets should protrude from the jig by about ⅛ inch. Press the toggle clamps down on the top to secure the veneer sheets to the jig. Turn on the router and slide the jig across the table to cut the veneer *(left)*, keeping the jig pressed against the pilot throughout the operation.

UNDERCUTTING CURVED EDGES

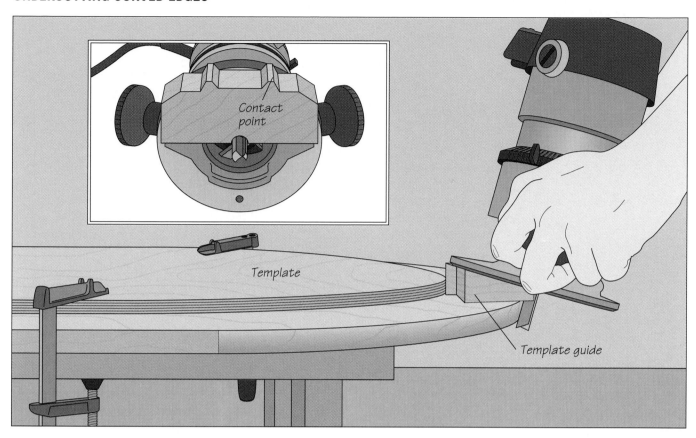

Contact point

Template

Template guide

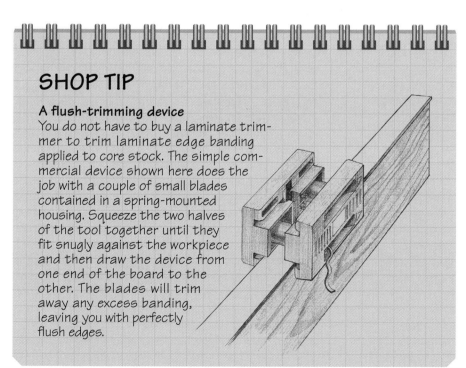

SHOP TIP

A flush-trimming device

You do not have to buy a laminate trimmer to trim laminate edge banding applied to core stock. The simple commercial device shown here does the job with a couple of small blades contained in a spring-mounted housing. Squeeze the two halves of the tool together until they fit snugly against the workpiece and then draw the device from one end of the board to the other. The blades will trim away any excess banding, leaving you with perfectly flush edges.

Using a shop-made template guide

This technique enables you to undercut the perimeter of a circular workpiece using a straight bit. To make the guide, cut a bevel across the face of a wood block. Make the width of the guide equal to the distance between the bit and the edge of the router sub-base. Saw two triangular contact points 1 inch apart in the guide's outside edge *(inset)*; also cut a notch out of the inside edge to accommodate the bit. Install a straight bit in the router and screw the jig to the router's base. Clamp a template atop the workpiece so that the distance between the template and the workpiece's edge is the same as that between the bit and the contact points of the guide. Make the cut *(above)*, keeping the contact points flush against the template throughout the operation. Reposition the template as necessary to finish the cut.

JOINTING ON A ROUTER TABLE

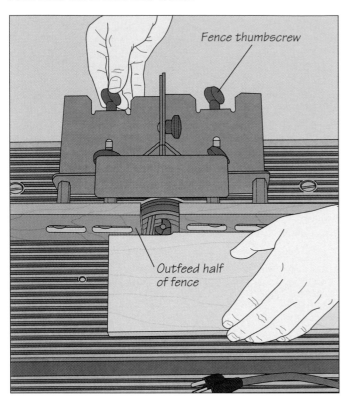

Fence thumbscrew

Outfeed half
of fence

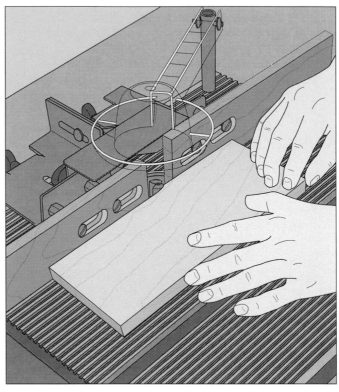

Jointing an edge

Install a straight bit in the router with a cutting edge longer than the thickness of your workpiece, and mount the tool in a router table. To remove $\frac{1}{16}$ inch of wood from your stock—a typical amount when jointing—adjust the position of the fence for a cut of that amount. Make a test cut in a scrap board, then unplug the router and hold the board in place against the fence. Loosen the outfeed fence thumbscrews and advance the outfeed half until it butts against the cut part of the board *(above, left)*. Tighten the thumbscrews. Butt the workpiece against the fence a few inches back from the bit and then slowly feed the board into the cutter, keeping your hand clear of the bit and pressing the workpiece firmly against the fence *(above, right)*. Apply side pressure just to the outfeed side of the bit. For narrow stock, finish the cut with a push stick.

SHOP TIP

Jointing wide boards
If you have boards that are too cumbersome to move across the jointer, you can undertake the task with a router and a perfectly square edge guide. Install a $\frac{1}{2}$-inch top-piloted flush-trimming bit in a router with a $\frac{1}{2}$-inch collet. Position the edge guide atop the board to be jointed and clamp the pieces to a workbench with the edge of the board protruding from the guide's edge by about $\frac{1}{16}$ inch. Feed the router from one end of the board to the other; the pilot will ride along the guide as the cutter trims the board flush.

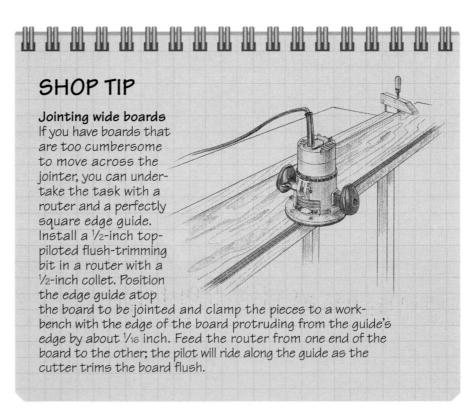

RAISING PANELS

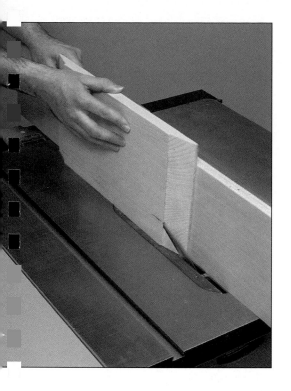

Frame-and-panel construction is a clever way of getting around the fact that wood shrinks and swells with changes in humidity. The principle is simple: The panel "floats" within the frame, sitting in grooves cut around its inside edges. Cutting a bevel around the edge of the panel allows the piece to fit into the grooves in the frame and gives a decorative "raised" effect to the main part of the panel.

Traditionally, panels were raised with special planes that featured angled and profiled cutters and soles. That job could

Panels can be raised on a number of stationary woodworking tools; a table saw with a tilting arbor works well. An auxiliary wood fence makes the job safer and more accurate.

require hours of arduous work, especially if the wood was dense, such as oak, maple, or cherry. Today you can raise panels on the table saw, radial arm saw, drill press, and shaper.

Panel raising is often done on the router table with one of several specially designed router bits *(page 48)*. These cutters can handle stock up to ¾ inch thick, but the bits' large diameter—typically 3½ inches—can make the workpiece difficult to control. If you plan to do a lot of panel raising, consider building a jig for the task *(page 50)*.

Since raising panels involves removal of a good deal of stock, it is best not to attempt to make the cut in one pass. Instead, make a series of partial passes, increasing the depth of cut gradually each time, until the panel is ¼ inch thick at the edges or fits snugly in the grooves cut in the frame.

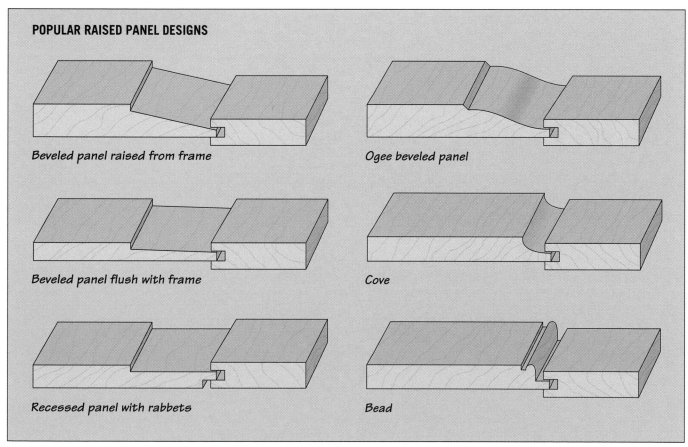

POPULAR RAISED PANEL DESIGNS

Beveled panel raised from frame

Ogee beveled panel

Beveled panel flush with frame

Cove

Recessed panel with rabbets

Bead

RAISING PANELS ON THE ROUTER TABLE

Using a piloted panel-raising bit

Install a piloted panel-raising bit in your router and mount the tool in a router table. With the router turned off, loosen the four fence adjustment screws and move the two halves of the fence as close as possible to the bit without touching the cutting edges. Tighten the screws. To ensure that the width of cut is uniform, position the fence in line with the edge of the bit pilot: Loosen the thumbscrews behind the fence, then hold a straightedge against the fence and move both halves together until the straightedge contacts the pilot. The pilot should turn as the edge touches it *(right, above)*; adjust the fence's position, if necessary, then tighten the thumbscrews. Set the router for a ⅛-inch depth of cut, lower the guard over the bit and turn on the router. For added stability, you can clamp a featherboard to each half of the fence to press the panel against the table. (In the illustrations on this page, the featherboards have been removed for clarity.) To minimize tearout, cut into the end grain of the panel first, beveling the ends before the sides. With the outside face of the panel down on the table, feed the stock into the bit, pushing it forward with your right hand and keeping it flush against the fence with your left *(right, below)*. Test-fit the panel in the frame grooves and make subsequent passes, increasing the cutting depth by a maximum of ⅛ inch each time.

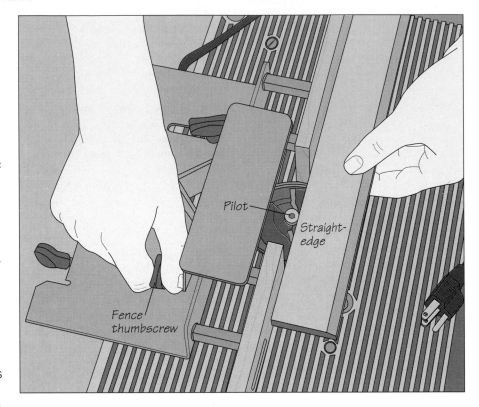

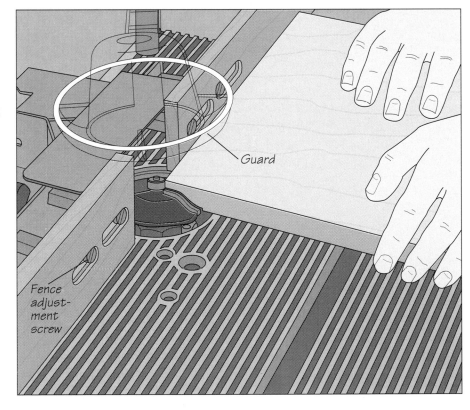

Using a non-piloted vertical panel-raising bit

In this operation, the panel will be fed across the bit in an upright position, so you must attach a high auxiliary wood fence *(right)*. Make the fence about 8 inches high and cut a notch in the middle to accommodate the bit. For this cut, the cutting depth depends on the amount by which the bit protrudes from the fence. To begin, set the fence for a ⅛-inch depth of cut. To secure the panel, clamp a featherboard to the table; rest the featherboard on a shim to keep the panel from tilting as you run it past the bit. Feed the panel with your right hand while pressing it flat against the fence with your left *(below)*. Cut the top and bottom of the panel first, then the sides. Back the fence from the bit no more than ⅛ inch at a time for further, deeper passes until the panel fits into the groove.

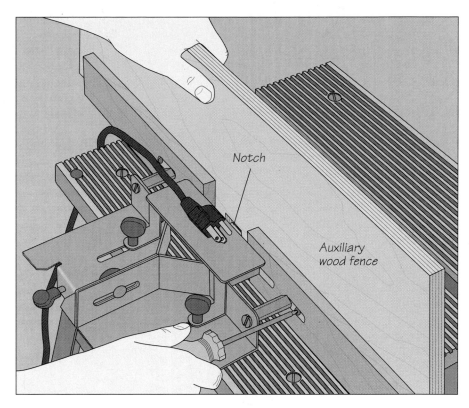

Notch

Auxiliary wood fence

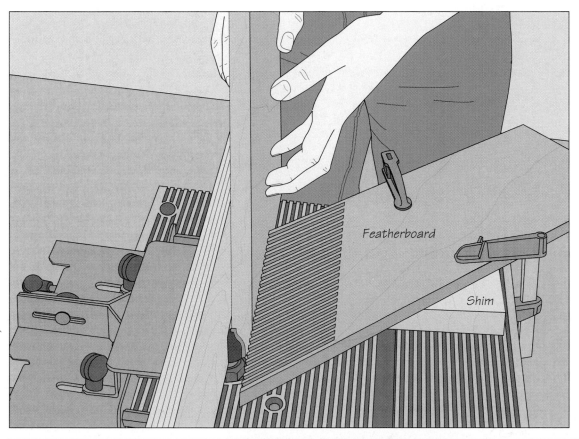

Featherboard

Shim

BUILD IT YOURSELF

A PANEL-RAISING JIG

The shop-made jig at right allows you to raise panels without mounting your router in a table. Featuring a tilting table and a fence to which the router is attached, the jig is secured to a workbench tail vise. This provides a safe, accurate way to mill a wide range of profiles.

Cut all the pieces of the jig from ¾-inch plywood; the dimensions suggested in the illustration will work well with the typical workbench. Start assembling the jig by screwing the brackets to the underside of the table at one end. Cut adjustment slots through the arms, then bolt the top ends of the arms to the brackets and the bottom ends to the fence using hanger bolts, washers, and wing nuts. Attach the table to the fence with a piano hinge positioned about 6 inches below the top of the fence. To prepare the fence for your router, bore a hole just above the table level that will accom-

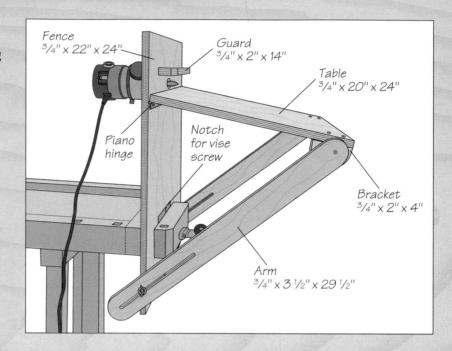

Fence
¾" x 22" x 24"

Guard
¾" x 2" x 14"

Table
¾" x 20" x 24"

Piano
hinge

Notch
for vise
screw

Bracket
¾" x 2" x 4"

Arm
¾" x 3 ½" x 29 ½"

modate your largest vertical panel-raising bit. Screw the guard to the fence above the hole. Finally, cut a notch into the bottom end of the fence to clear the vise screw.

To use the jig, secure it in the vise so the table is at a comfortable working height. Install a ½-inch vertical panel-raising bit in the router, then screw the base plate to the fence so the bit protrudes from the hole. Adjusting the bit for a shallow cut, turn on the router and make a test cut in a scrap piece. To adjust the bevel angle, turn off the tool, loosen the wing nuts securing the arms to the fence and tilt the table up or down. As on the router table, cut the bevels on the ends of the panel before those on the sides. Feed the panel across the table face-up *(left)*, keeping your fingers clear of the bit. Test-fit the panel and increase the cutting depth by ⅛ inch for a second pass.

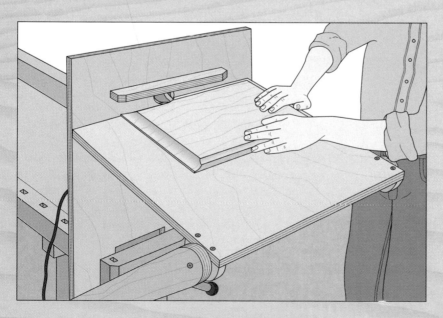

RAISING PANELS ON THE DRILL PRESS

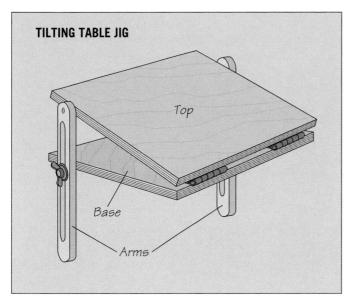

TILTING TABLE JIG

Top

Base

Arms

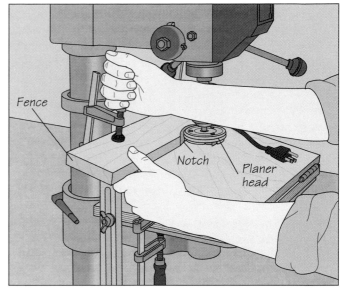

Fence

Notch

Planer
head

1 Setting up the jig
Fitted with a planer head and a tilting table jig, a drill press can raise panels quickly and safely. Install the planer head in the chuck, adjusting the machine's drilling speed to the setting specified by the accessory's manufacturer. For the jig, cut the base and top from ¾-inch plywood, and join the pieces with butt hinges *(above, left)*. Cut the arms from 1-by-2 stock, then rout a slot through each one for a hang-

er bolt. Screw the arms to the top and then secure them to the base with hanger bolts, washers, and wing nuts. Clamp the base to the drill press table, loosen the wing nuts and set the top to the bevel angle you wish to cut. Tighten the wing nuts, then adjust the table height to position the top about 1 inch below the planer head. Cut a fence from solid stock, saw a notch out of one edge to clear the planer head, and clamp it to the top *(above, right)*.

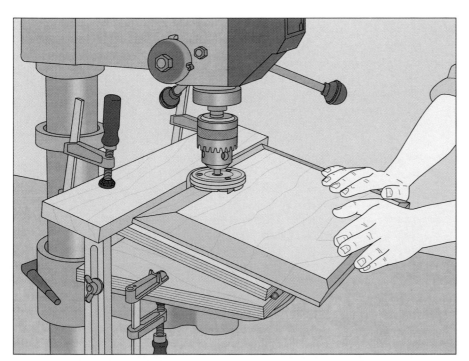

2 Raising the panel
Make a test cut on a scrap board. To change the bevel angle, adjust the arms to tilt the top of the jig. The depth of cut on your first pass should not exceed ⅛ inch. Lower the drill press table to decrease the cutting depth; raise the table to increase it. Run the panel face up past the planer head, keeping the workpiece flush against the fence with your left hand and pushing it forward with your right *(left)*. To minimize tearout, start by beveling the ends before the sides. For additional passes, increase the cutting depth ⅛ inch at a time.

MAKING MOLDINGS

Routers and shapers are most often chosen to cut moldings, and the use of the table-mounted router for this purpose is shown on page 57.

However, your table saw or radial arm saw is also an excellent choice for cutting moldings. By replacing the saw blade with a molding head and interchangeable cutters, you can reproduce an impressive array of designs. Some of the cutter profiles available for these saws are illustrated below, together with the cuts they produce. The techniques for using them are explained on pages 53 and 54.

Page 55 presents a jig you can make for cutting cove molding in a remarkably simple fashion—on a table saw.

Molding operations can be hazardous. The cutters strike with great force, and are capable of causing severe kickback and inflicting serious wounds.

Two principal safety rules apply to saws and routers. No single cut should be deeper than ⅛ inch; many shallow passes will produce superior results and reduce the risk of kickback. To ensure adequate control over your work, never mold stock that is shorter than 12 inches or narrower than 4 inches. If narrow molding is required, it can be ripped from wider stock when the shaping operation is complete.

A final safety tip pertains to routers: Because molding bits are generally larger and heavier than ordinary bits, molding operations are often best conducted with the tool mounted in a table. This frees both hands to control your work.

Installed in a table-mounted router, this traditional molding bit can transform a plain board into an elaborate molding.

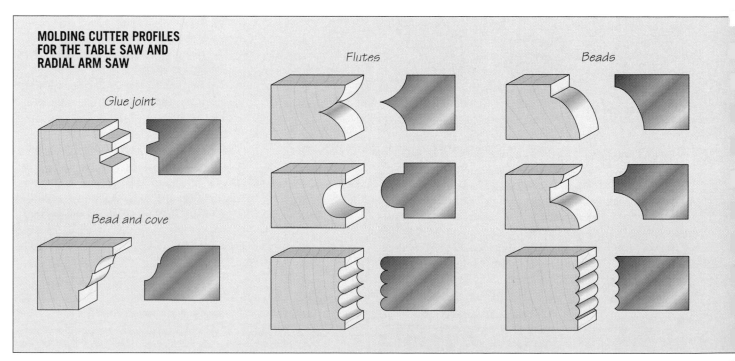

MOLDING CUTTER PROFILES FOR THE TABLE SAW AND RADIAL ARM SAW

Glue joint

Bead and cove

Flutes

Beads

CUTTING MOLDING ON THE TABLE SAW

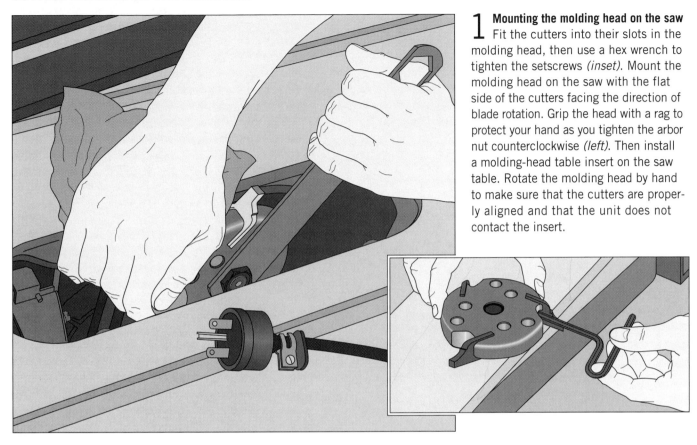

1 Mounting the molding head on the saw
Fit the cutters into their slots in the molding head, then use a hex wrench to tighten the setscrews *(inset)*. Mount the molding head on the saw with the flat side of the cutters facing the direction of blade rotation. Grip the head with a rag to protect your hand as you tighten the arbor nut counterclockwise *(left)*. Then install a molding-head table insert on the saw table. Rotate the molding head by hand to make sure that the cutters are properly aligned and that the unit does not contact the insert.

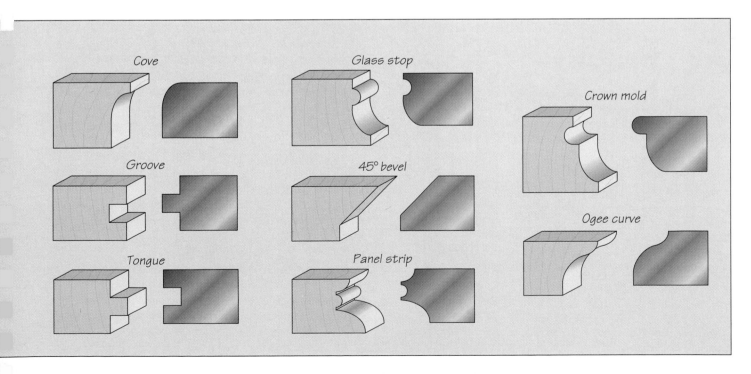

Cove

Glass stop

Crown mold

Groove

45° bevel

Tongue

Panel strip

Ogee curve

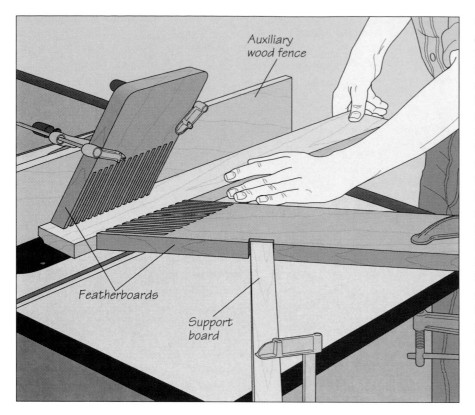

Auxiliary
wood fence

Featherboards

Support
board

2 Making the first pass

Install an auxiliary wood fence and position it over the molding head. Keeping the metal fence clear of the cutters, cut a clearance notch by gradually raising the cutterhead into the fence. Turn off the saw and position the fence for the profile you want. Secure the workpiece with two featherboards, one clamped to the fence above the blade, and a second fixed to the saw table. Clamp a support board at a 90° angle to the second featherboard. Place a shim behind the featherboard on the fence, if necessary, to prevent the workpiece from tilting during the cut. Raise the cutters only ⅛ inch above the table; do not make a full-depth cut in one pass. To make the cut, slowly feed the workpiece into the cutters with your right hand, pressing it against the fence with your left hand *(left)*. Finish the cut with a push stick. Reverse the board and repeat the cut on the other edge.

3 Making the final pass

Make as many passes as necessary, raising the molding head ⅛ inch at a time, until you have reached the desired depth of cut. For the final pass, raise the molding head very slightly and pass the workpiece across the cutters very slowly, feeding it with a push stick as the board's trailing end approaches the cutters *(right)*. This will produce a smooth finish that will require little sanding. Once the proper profile has been cut, remove the molding cutter head from the saw and install a rip or combination blade to cut the molding from both sides of the workpiece.

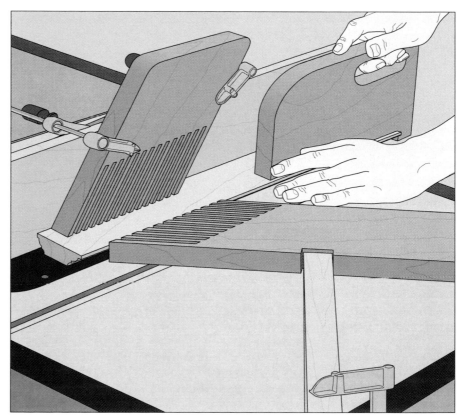

BUILD IT YOURSELF

A COVE CUTTING GUIDE

Cutting coves on a table saw is essentially simple: The concave shape is easily formed by moving the work across a partially raised blade at an angle. However, accurately setting up the saw to achieve the proper angle, width, and depth of cut can be tricky.

The task is simplified by using the cove cutting guide shown below,

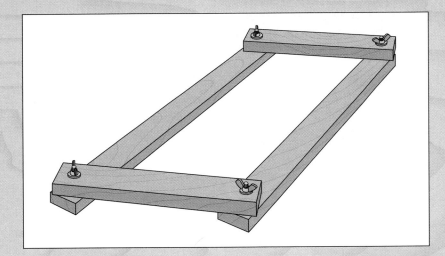

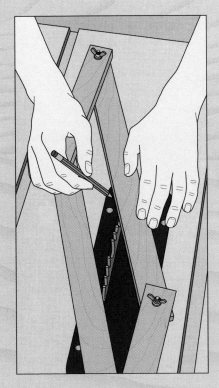

consisting of four 2-inch-wide strips of ¾-inch hardwood or plywood, assembled to form a parallelogram roughly 18 inches long by 9 inches wide. The pieces are fastened with countersunk machine screws and wing nuts for easy adjustment.

Here is how to use it: Set the distance between the jig's long sides to the width of the cove and tighten the wing nuts. Raise the saw blade to the desired depth of cut, then lay the jig over the blade.

Position the jig so that its edges lightly contact the blade. This will be the angle at which your work must cross the blade to produce the desired cove. Use a pencil or china marker to trace guidelines on the saw table *(left)*. Remove the jig, place it on your workpiece, and mark similar guidelines on the leading end.

Lower the blade and set the workpiece on the saw table, aligning both sets of guidelines. It will require some care to make sure that the board edges are parallel to the guidelines. When they are, butt guide boards against the stock and clamp them in place. Check the alignment of the boards and begin your cut.

Each pass should be no more than ⅛ inch deep. Feed the board slowly, using push blocks throughout the operation *(below)*. For a smooth finish, make a final pass at half the depth and speed as the previous passes.

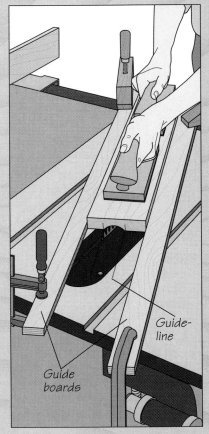

Guide-line

Guide boards

BUILD IT YOURSELF

AN AUXILIARY TABLE FOR THE RADIAL ARM SAW

If you want to cut molding on the radial arm saw with the molding head in the horizontal position, try an auxiliary table like the one shown below. With the saw arbor in the vertical position, the molding head cannot be lowered to the level of the standard table.

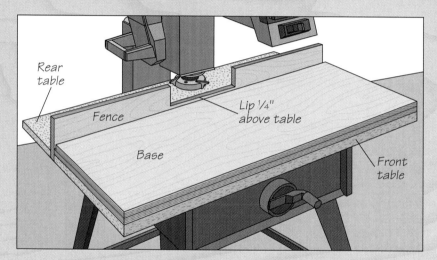

Rear table

Fence

Base

Lip ¼" above table

Front table

The auxiliary base raises the workpiece to the cutters, and the fence supports the work while providing a clearance cutout for the cutters and molding head guard.

Cut the two pieces for the jig base from ¾-inch plywood; make them the same size as the front saw table. Screw the pieces together, offsetting the top slightly to create a gap along the fence that will prevent sawdust from accumulating between the base of the auxiliary table and the fence when the jig is in position. Cut the fence from ¾-inch plywood, making it about 5 inches wide. When sawing the cutout for the molding head guard, leave a lip that will

protrude at least ¼ inch above the table when the jig is installed. The lip will support the workpiece as it rides along the fence during a cut.

To install the auxiliary table, screw the fence to the base, slip the fence between the front and rear saw tables, then tighten the table clamps to secure the jig in place.

Fit a molding head to the saw arbor as you would with a table saw *(page 53)*; install a plastic guard on the molding head to protect your hands during the cuts. To secure the workpiece, clamp two featherboards to the fence on either side of the molding head and a third featherboard to the table, bracing it with a support board. Set a ⅛-inch cutting depth and turn on the saw. Feed the stock slowly into the molding head with your right hand *(below)*; use your left hand to press the workpiece against the fence. Finish the pass with a push stick. Make as many passes as necessary, advancing the molding head only ⅛ inch farther into the workpiece at a time. Once you have cut the desired profile, make a final, very shallow pass, feeding more slowly to help produce a smooth finish.

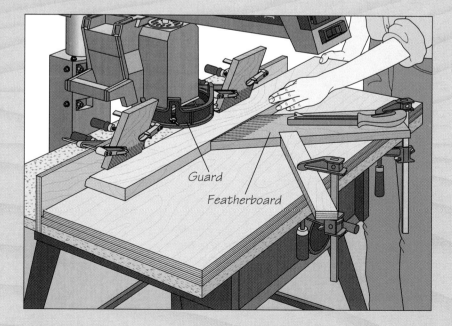

Guard

Featherboard

MOLDING ON THE ROUTER TABLE

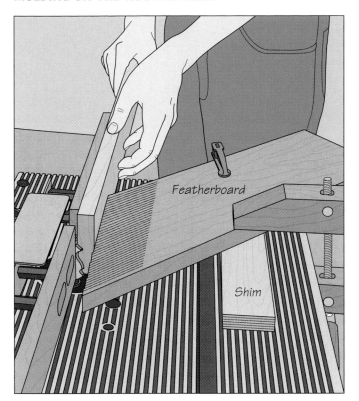

Featherboard

Shim

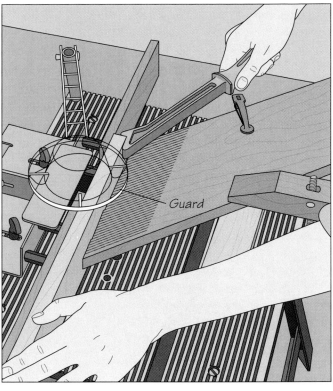

Guard

SHOP TIP

A miter gauge for the router table
If your router table does not have a miter gauge slot, you can build a simple device to guide stock across the table while keeping it square to the fence. The jig consists of an L-shaped support piece and a guide that rides along the front edge of the table. To use the jig, butt the end of the workpiece against the fence while holding its edge against the support piece. Then push the workpiece and the gauge together into the bit.

Routing a molding

Install a molding bit in your router and mount the tool in a table. If you are using a large bit, adjust the fence for a shallow cut—about ⅛ inch; do not attempt to rout the full profile in one pass. To hold the workpiece in place, clamp a featherboard to the table in line with the bit; raise the featherboard with a wood shim so that it supports the middle of the workpiece. With your stock clear of the bit, turn on the router and slowly feed the workpiece into the cutting edge while holding it flush against the fence *(above, left)*. **(Caution: Guard in this illustration removed for clarity.)** To keep your hands safely away from the bit, finish the pass with a push stick *(above, right)*. Make as many passes as necessary to rout the desired profile, increasing the cutting depth by ⅛ inch at a time.

PIN ROUTING

Pin routing takes its name from the steel pin or pins that guide the workpiece across a cutting tool that is mounted above the work table. Non-piloted bits can be used for some cuts, and the technique is particularly useful for following a template *(page 61)*. Piloted bits can also be used, as can an auxiliary fence *(page 59)*.

The assembly shown at right combines the features of a shaper, a drill press, and a router table. Like a drill press, the business end of the assembly (in this case, a portable electric router) is mounted in a carriage above the table. The cutting edge is above the work—a common setup on the shaper. The pin routing attachment features a depth adjustment lever that, much like a drill press feed lever, raises and lowers the bit to the desired depth of cut.

The assembly enables you to produce edge profiles ranging from chamfers to crown moldings; it also works well cutting mortises, tenons, and rabbets.

Suspended above a sturdy work table in this commercial pin routing attachment, the portable router becomes a stationary shaping tool for intricate edge-forming operations.

SETTING UP A PIN ROUTING ASSEMBLY

Mounting the router in the attachment

With the appropriate bit in the router, install the tool in the pin routing attachment following the manufacturer's instructions. Secure the router in the carriage by tightening the lock nut *(right)*. Next set the depth of cut. This depends on the distance between the bit and the table—typically 2 to 3 inches, depending on the thickness of your workpiece. Pull down on the depth control handle to lower the carriage and the bit as far as they will go; movement of the carriage will stop when the depth stop rod contacts the assembly housing. To adjust the depth of the cut, loosen the wing nut on the depth stop rod, then turn the rod clockwise to increase the cutting depth; counterclockwise to decrease it. Tighten the wing nut.

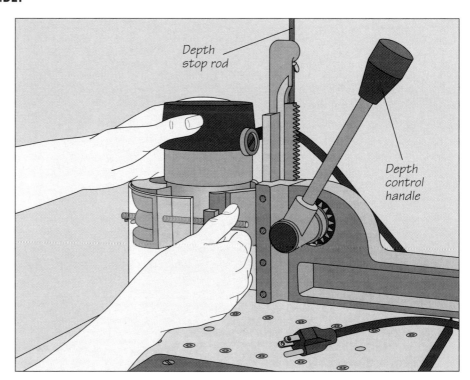

Depth stop rod

Depth control handle

STRAIGHT AND CURVED ROUTING

Shaping a straight edge

Make straight cuts on the pin routing attachment using a non-piloted bit and a fence. Cut an auxiliary wood fence as long as the table, notch it to accommodate the bit, and screw it to the table's fence. Install two featherboards to hold the work securely; the type shown slides in the miter slot. Follow the manufacturer's instructions for positioning the workpiece and setting the width of cut. On the table illustrated, the entire top is moved to adjust the width of cut. Lower the guard so that it is no more than ¼ inch above the workpiece, then turn on the router. Feed the stock against the direction of bit rotation, pressing it against the fence *(right)*. Finish the pass with a push stick.

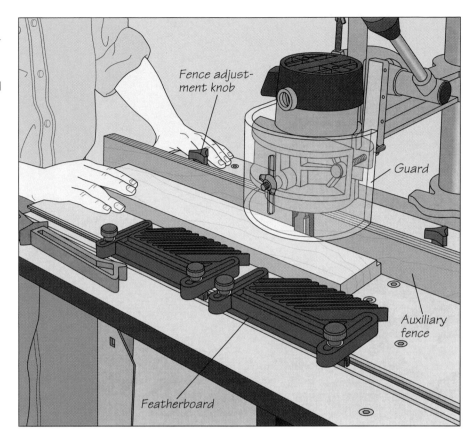

Fence adjust-
ment knob

Guard

Auxiliary
fence

Featherboard

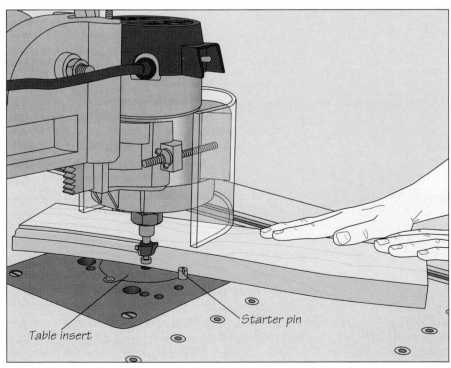

Table insert

Starter pin

Forming a curved edge

A piloted bit makes it easy to follow the contour of a workpiece. After mounting the table insert, place the starter pin in its hole on the infeed side of the bit. As you feed the workpiece into the cutting edges, brace the stock against the starter pin *(left)*. Make sure you keep the workpiece flush against the bit pilot and your hands clear of the cutter.

CONTOURED CUTS WITH NON-PILOTED BITS

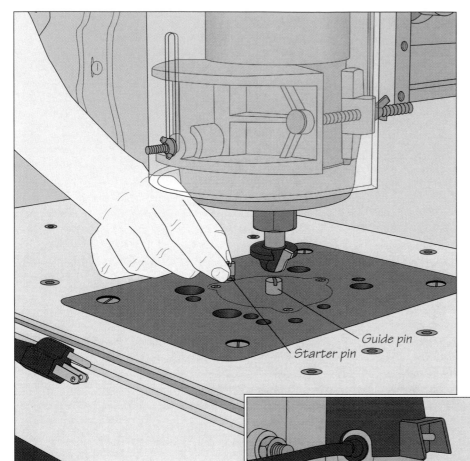

Guide pin

Starter pin

1 Installing the guide pin and starter pin

To shape a curved edge using a non-piloted bit, screw a guide pin into the center hole of the table insert. The attachment shown comes with guide pins of three different diameters: $\frac{1}{4}$, $\frac{3}{8}$, and $\frac{1}{2}$ inch; a smaller pin will produce a wider cut. Then install the starter pin in the table on the infeed side of the bit *(left)*.

2 Shaping the contour

Once the pins are installed, adjust the tabletop as you would for a straight cut *(page 59)* so the guide pin is directly under the bit. As you start the cut, brace the workpiece against the starter pin. Once the bit cuts into the stock and the guide pin contacts the wood, move the workpiece off the starter pin to continue the cut *(right)*. Keep the stock butted against the guide pin throughout the operation.

SHAPING CURVES WITH A TEMPLATE

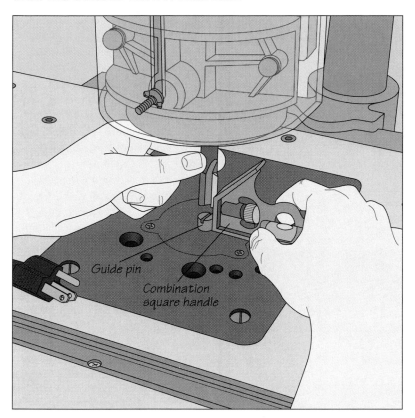

Guide pin

Combination
square handle

Making and using a template

A template and a non-piloted straight bit allow you to accurately finish a curved edge with a pin routing setup. Start by installing a bit and guide pin of the same diameter. Adjust the tabletop to position the guide pin directly under the bit. Check that the pin is perfectly aligned with the bit using the handle of a combination square *(left)*. Install the starter pin on the infeed side of the bit. After you have made a plywood template, rough-cut the workpiece to size as you would for a pattern-routing operation *(page 38)*. Use double-sided tape to fasten your stock atop the template. In making the cut, brace the template against the starter pin, then press it toward the guide pin. Once the template touches the guide pin and the bit starts cutting, pivot the stock off the starter pin. Continue the cut, keeping the template flush against the guide pin *(below)*.

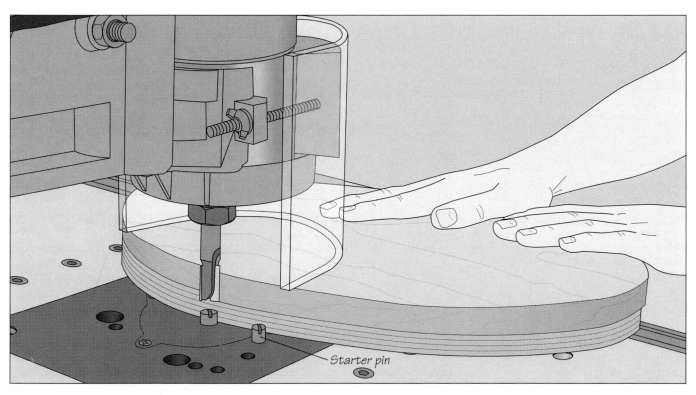

Starter pin

ROUTING INSIDE EDGES

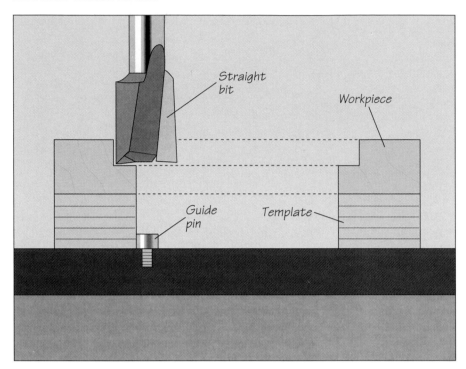

Straight bit

Workpiece

Guide pin

Template

1 Setting up
A template and guide pin can also be used to shape an inside edge with a non-piloted straight bit. The illustrations on this page show how to cut a rabbet along the inside edge of an oval picture frame. Mount a guide pin that is smaller than the bit; the width of the rabbet will equal one-half the difference between the two diameters; for example, a ¾-inch bit paired with a ¼-inch guide pin will yield a ¼-inch-wide rabbet *(left)*. Adjust the tabletop to position the guide pin directly under the bit and install the starter pin on the infeed side of the table—which, for routing an inside edge, is on the right-hand side of the guide pin. Make a template, cut your workpiece to the same dimensions as the pattern, and fasten the stock atop the template.

2 Routing the rabbet
Be sure to adjust the cutting depth *(page 58)* for the depth of the rabbet. Turn on the router with the template and the workpiece clear of the bit. Then make the cut, guiding the template and work-piece in a counterclockwise direction from the starter pin to the guide pin. Continue rotating the workpiece *(right)*, keeping the template butted firmly against the guide pin.

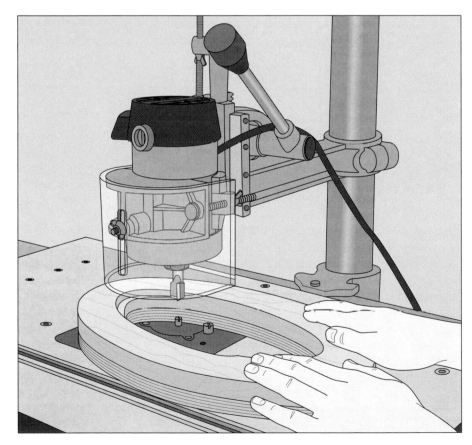

BUILD IT YOURSELF

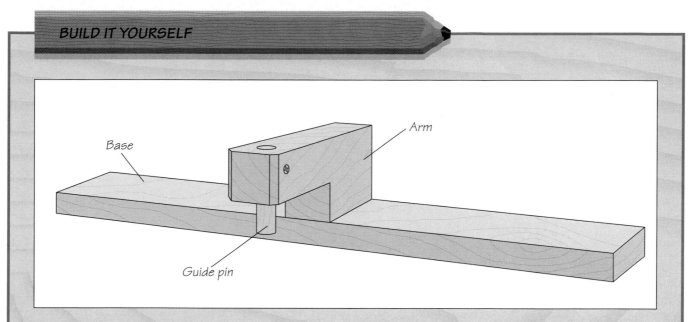

Base

Arm

Guide pin

PIN ROUTING ON A ROUTER TABLE

You can perform most of the pin routing operations featured on pages 58 to 62 using a conventional router table and the shop-built jig shown above. The setup stands conventional pin routing on its head. Rather than suspending the router over a guide pin, the tool is mounted upside down in a router table and the guide pin is positioned over the bit.

The jig affords two advantages over commercial arrangements. First, a router is safer when it is fixed under a table; second, the guide pin is more visible when it is held above the work surface.

Cut the base of the jig from hardwood; make it as long as your router table. The L-shaped arm, also of hardwood, should be long enough so that it extends over the bit when its back edge is flush with the back of the router table and the jig base. Screw the arm to the base. For the guide pin, bore a ½-inch-diameter hole through the arm and glue a piece of dowel in place; cut the dowel so it will sit at least 1 inch

above the surface of the table. Drive a screw into one side of the arm to secure the dowel in position.

To use the jig, install the appropriate bit in the router and mount the tool in the table. Clamp the base of the jig to the table so the guide

pin is directly above the bit. Shape an edge as you would in conventional pin routing *(page 61)*, except the template should sit atop the workpiece *(below)*. Make sure you butt the template against the guide pin throughout the operation.

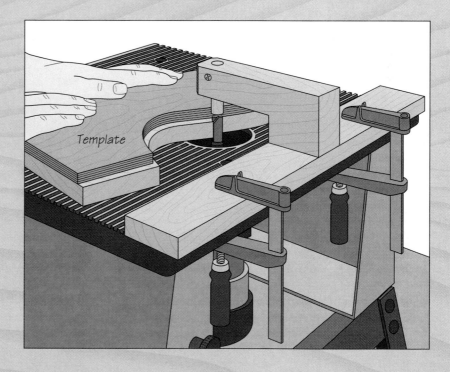

Template

SPEED SELECTION CHART

MAT'L	CUTTER SIZE			
	1/4	3/8	1/2	3/4
SOFT	F	D-E	C-D	B-C
MEDIUM	E	D-E	C-D	B-C
HARD	E-E	C	C	B-C
VERY HARD	D	A-B	C	B

■ DOUBLE INSULATED   ■ 10,000-25,000 R.P.M.
110/120 VOLTS AC ONLY, 60 Hz 15 AMPS

WARNING: FOR SAFE OPERATION SEE OWNERS MANUAL.
WEAR EYE PROTECTION. FOR SERVICING USE ONLY
IDENTICAL CRAFTSMAN REPLACEMENT PARTS.

A2340   ELECTRONIC PLUNGE ROUTER
MODEL 315.275060
Sears, Roebuck and Co.   MADE IN U.S.A.

GROOVING

A core box bit carves a circular groove near the edge of a walnut tabletop. To ensure that this decorative cut follows the arc of the workpiece, a curved extension is fastened to a commercial edge guide to ride along the edge of the stock.

Although basic router techniques remain essentially unchanged no matter what the operation, cutting grooves involves special skills, whether the cuts are intended to be ornamental or functional.

This chapter demonstrates the tools and techniques used to rout a wide assortment of grooves, from the simple dadoes used to assemble carcases and cabinets to recesses for inlays and the graceful patterns that can form the decorative focus of a piece of furniture.

Many techniques will be used frequently, as the cuts are essential to most projects; others, although perhaps less commonly used, will allow you to extend the scope of your work and improve the level of your craftsmanship.

The best router to use depends on the task at hand. Although a standard router will perform virtually every job adequately, a plunge router is preferred for interior cuts, such as routing stopped grooves *(page 69)* or cutting recesses for inlay *(page 86)*, since it allows you to align the bit over the cut and plunge it into the stock.

For safety and precision, it is often best to mount your router in a table *(page 75)*. A router table affords a high degree of control that makes it a relatively simple task to rout stopped grooves and rabbets.

On page 81 we show techniques for following a predetermined pattern, and on page 84 you will find a discussion of pin routing for cutting grooves.

Whether your router has plunging capabilities or not, and whether or not it is mounted in a table, you will be using a wide variety of accessories—jigs, bits, cutters, guides, and templates—that ease the completion of certain tasks and make others possible. A selection of commercial accessories is shown on page 66. Throughout this chapter you will find illustrated instructions for building your own accessories.

With these—and a little knowledge and imagination—you can make your router one of your most valuable tools.

Fitted with a straight bit, a router cuts a dado for a shelf in a carcase side panel— with the help of a commercial edge guide.

A GALLERY OF GROOVES AND ACCESSORIES

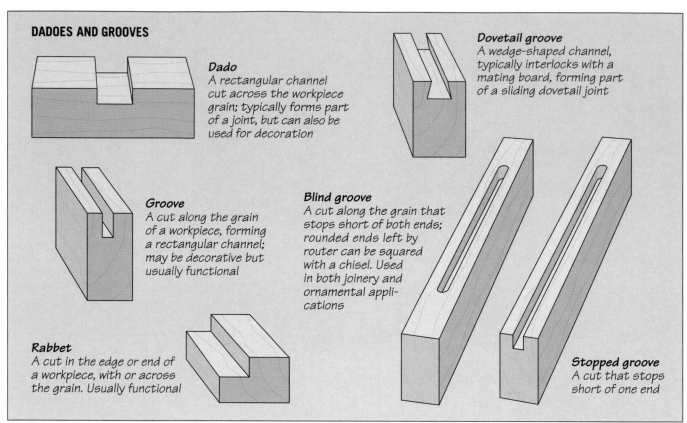

DADOES AND GROOVES

Dado
A rectangular channel cut across the workpiece grain; typically forms part of a joint, but can also be used for decoration

Dovetail groove
A wedge-shaped channel, typically interlocks with a mating board, forming part of a sliding dovetail joint

Groove
A cut along the grain of a workpiece, forming a rectangular channel; may be decorative but usually functional

Blind groove
A cut along the grain that stops short of both ends; rounded ends left by router can be squared with a chisel. Used in both joinery and ornamental applications

Rabbet
A cut in the edge or end of a workpiece, with or across the grain. Usually functional

Stopped groove
A cut that stops short of one end

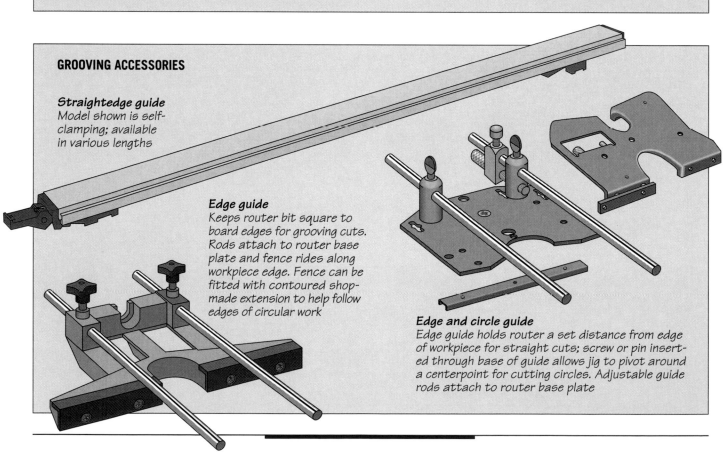

GROOVING ACCESSORIES

Straightedge guide
Model shown is self-clamping; available in various lengths

Edge guide
Keeps router bit square to board edges for grooving cuts. Rods attach to router base plate and fence rides along workpiece edge. Fence can be fitted with contoured shop-made extension to help follow edges of circular work

Edge and circle guide
Edge guide holds router a set distance from edge of workpiece for straight cuts; screw or pin inserted through base of guide allows jig to pivot around a centerpoint for cutting circles. Adjustable guide rods attach to router base plate

BUILD IT YOURSELF

ADJUSTABLE CIRCLE-CUTTING JIG

The shop-made jig shown below allows the router to cut circles of any diameter. Size the pieces of the jig to suit the job at hand. The center block can be cut from ¾-inch-thick stock; make it about 3 inches wide and 6 inches long. The diameter of the hardwood dowels depends on the size of the predrilled holes in the base plate of your router; cut the dowels longer than the radius of the largest circle you expect to rout.

To assemble the jig, slip the dowels into the holes in the router base plate, then set the tool flat on a work surface. Butt one edge of the center block against the ends of the dowels and mark the two points where the rods contact the edge. Bore a hole halfway through the block at each point, then spread a little glue in the holes and insert the dowels. Fix them in place with brads. Next, mark the center of the block and bore a hole through it for a screw.

To set up the cut, place your stock on the work surface. Butt wood scraps against the edges of the workpiece to act as cleats, then screw them in place. Mark the radius of the circle and its centerpoint. Install a straight bit in the router and set the cutting depth. For a deep cut, make several shallow passes.

To use the jig, attach the block to the center of the circle and slide the dowels along the router base plate until the edge of the bit closest to the circle's center is aligned with the end of the marked radius. Tighten the screws in the base plate to hold the dowels in place. Then rout the circle, feeding the router in a clockwise direction (below).

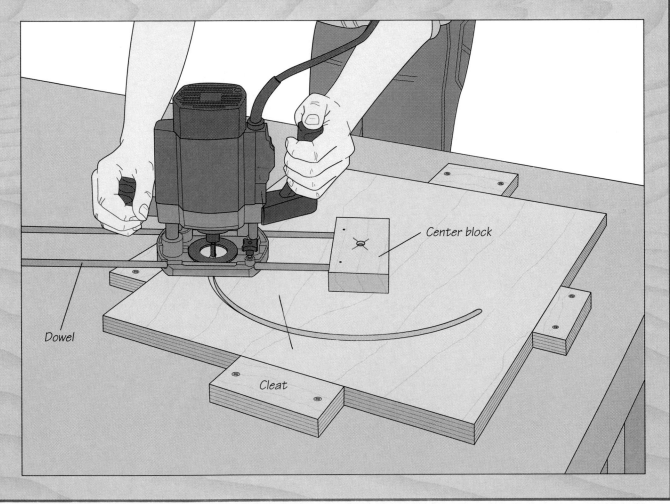

Center block

Dowel

Cleat

DADO CUTS

At one time, cutting dadoes cleanly and accurately was a painstaking task involving a specially designed hand plane or a saw and a wood chisel. Today, a router fitted with a straight bit can make quick work of any dado cut.

Whether you are routing a dado or a groove, the maximum depth of a single pass will depend on the hardness of the stock and the size of your router. In general, deep channels in hardwood require several passes. For cuts whose width exceeds the diameter of the bits you have on hand, make a series of passes. Three adjacent passes with a ½-inch bit, for example, will carve a dado or groove up to 1½ inches wide. (Usually, however, it would be better to make four slightly narrower cuts.)

A straight bit carves a groove in a board. Riding an edge guide along the board produces a cut parallel to the edge.

The following pages display several useful dadoing jigs. For cuts close to the edge of a workpiece, the edge guide supplied with the router is a helpful tool, as shown in the photograph at left. For cuts farther in from the edge, use a commercial or shop-built straightedge guide. As shown on page 69, stopped grooves are easy to cut using a straightedge and two stop blocks.

While any router will get the job done, a plunge router is best for making stopped dadoes and grooves. A standard router requires that you begin a stopped cut by tilting the base plate and pivoting the bit into the work; with a plunge router, you can hold the tool flat on the surface while plunging the bit straight into the wood.

CUTTING A GROOVE

Using an edge guide
Clamp your stock to a work surface, protecting the workpiece with wood pads, then mark the beginning of the groove on the face of the stock. Clamp an edge guide to the workpiece, using a tape measure to make certain the guide is the same distance from the cutting mark as the gap between the edge of the router base plate and the outermost part of the bit. The guide must be parallel to the workpiece edge. With a firm grip on the router, feed the bit into the stock at one end of the board, butting the tool's base plate against the edge guide *(right)*.

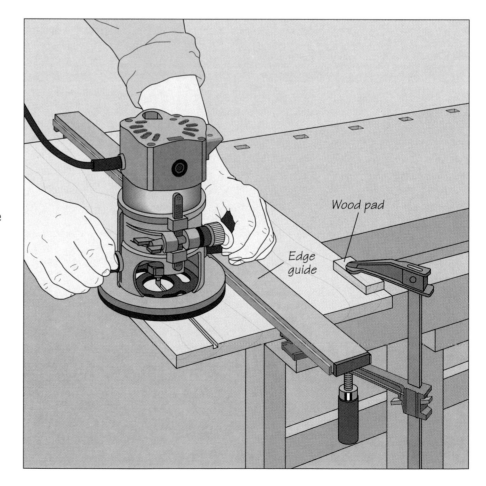

Wood pad

Edge guide

ROUTING A STOPPED GROOVE

Stop block

Edge guide

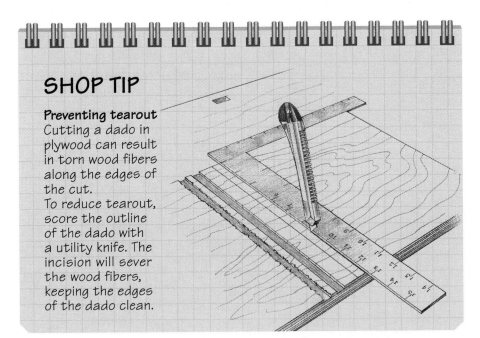

SHOP TIP

Preventing tearout
Cutting a dado in
plywood can result
in torn wood fibers
along the edges of
the cut.
To reduce tearout,
score the outline
of the dado with
a utility knife. The
incision will sever
the wood fibers,
keeping the edges
of the dado clean.

Using an edge guide and stop blocks
Set the stock on a work surface, then
center the bit over the cutting lines.
Clamp an edge guide to the workpiece
flush against the router base plate; check
that the guide is parallel to the edge
of the workpiece. Next align the bit
with one end of the marked lines and
clamp a stop block to the workpiece
flush with the router base plate.
Repeat the process at the other end of
the groove. To start the cut, rest the
base plate on the workpiece with the bit
clear of the stock and the plate butted
against the edge guide and one of the
stop blocks. Then plunge the bit into
the stock. Guide the router toward the
other stop block, keeping the base plate
flush against the edge guide (above).

ROUTING DADOES IN CARCASE SIDES

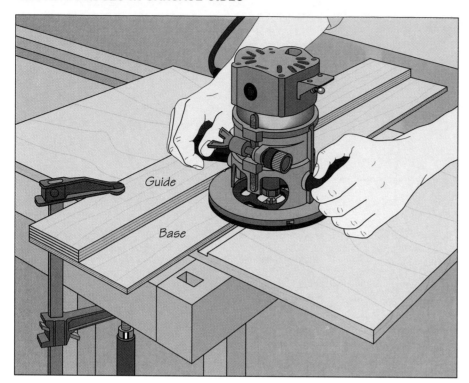

Making and using an edge guide
Made from two pieces of plywood, the shop-built jig shown at left enables you to make quick work of a dado cut. Since the distance between the guide and the edge of the base is the same as the gap between the edge of the router base plate and the bit, the jig can be quickly lined up with the dado outline. Cut the base from ¼-inch plywood and the guide from ¾-inch plywood; rip the pieces to widths to suit your router set up. Screw the two pieces together, making sure to countersink the fasteners. To rout the dado, set the stock on a work surface and clamp the edge guide atop the workpiece, aligning the edge of the jig base with the cutting marks. Set the router's cutting depth, remembering to account for the thickness of the base. Rout the channel *(left)*, keeping the base flush against the guide and flat on the base.

Cutting two dadoes in one pass
For a fixed shelf to sit level in a bookcase or cabinet, it must rest in dadoes at the same height in both side panels. One way to make certain the cuts line up is to rout both dadoes at the same time. Clamp the stock to a work surface, ensuring that the ends of the panels are aligned; protect the workpieces with wood pads. Then clamp an edge guide to the stock, positioning the jig so the router bit will line up directly over the dado outline *(page 68)*. Make certain that the edge guide is square to the panel edges. Rout the dado *(right)*.

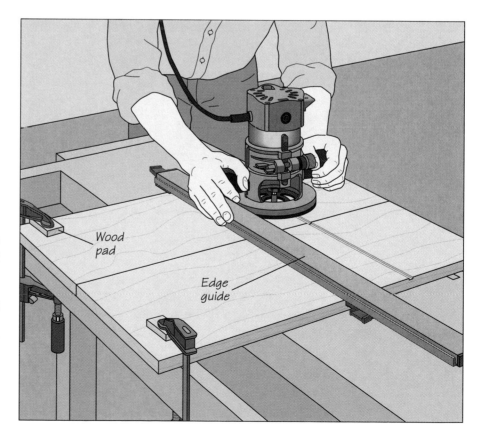

BUILD IT YOURSELF

T-SQUARE JIG FOR GROOVING

To rout dadoes and grooves that are straight and perfectly square to the edge of your stock, construct a T-square jig like the one shown at right, made from ¾-inch plywood.

Size the jig to accommodate the stock you will be using and the diameter of your router base plate. Make the edge guide about 4 inches wide and at least as long as the width of the workpiece; the fence, also about 4 inches wide, should extend on either side of the guide by about the width of the router base plate.

To assemble the jig, screw the fence to the edge guide with countersunk screws. Use a try square to make certain the two pieces are per-

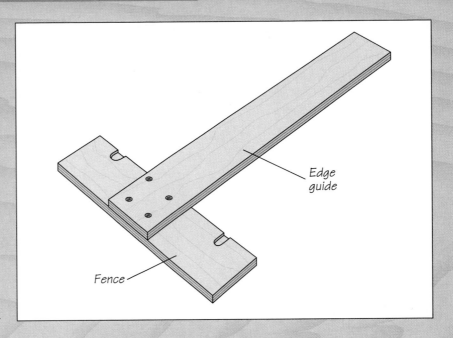

Edge guide

Fence

pendicular to each other. Then clamp the jig to a work surface and rout a short dado on each side of the fence, using your two most commonly used bits—often ½- and ¾-inch. These dadoes in the fence will minimize tearout when the jig is used, as well as serving to align the jig.

To use the jig, clamp it to the workpiece, aligning the appropriate dado in the fence with the outline on the stock. When making the cut, keep the router base plate firmly against the edge guide *(left)*. Continue the cut a short distance into the fence before stopping the router.

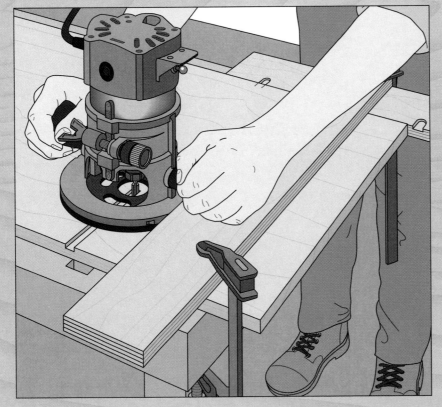

BUILD IT YOURSELF

QUICK-SETUP GROOVING JIG

Consisting of four strips of ¾-inch plywood assembled to form two Ls, the jig shown at right makes it easy to rout dadoes and grooves with minimal tearout. Make all the pieces of the jig about 4 inches wide. Cut the edge guides a few inches longer than the cut you intend to make. The cleats should be long enough to overlap the adjacent edge guide by several inches when the jig is set up. Attach the cleats to the edge guides, making sure that the pieces are perpendicular to each other; use four countersunk screws for each connection.

Set up the jig by clamping the stock to a work surface and butting the cleats against the workpiece at the beginning and end of the cut. Then set your router between the edge guides, aligning the bit over the dado outline. Slide the guides together until they butt against each side of the router base plate. Secure the jig by clamping it at opposing corners and to the workpiece. Then turn on the router and, with the tool between the edge guides, start the cut in the cleat, creating an entry dado. Guide the router across the workpiece *(right, below)*, extending the cut completely through the stock and into the second cleat. This will minimize tearout as the bit exits the workpiece. If you need to rout several dadoes of the same size, leave the jig clamped together and align the entry dado with the cutting lines marked on the stock.

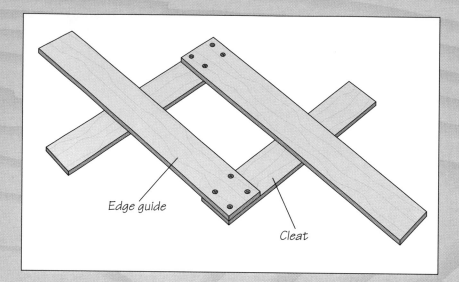

Edge guide

Cleat

Edge guide

Entry dado

Cleat

CUTTING GROOVES IN THIN STOCK

Guide block

Guide block

Grooving a narrow edge

To rout a groove along a surface that is too narrow to accommodate an edge guide, attach a short guide block to the router itself. Install a straight bit and set the router upside down on a work surface. Remove the sub-base if necessary and screw the guide block to the tool through one of the predrilled holes in the base plate. Mark the width of the groove on one end of the workpiece and align the marks with the bit. Then pivot the guide block until it is flush against the face of the stock. Clamp the guide to the base plate. Hold the marked end of the workpiece against the bit again to check that the guide is positioned properly *(above, left)*. To cut the groove, secure the workpiece edge up in a vise. Set the router flat on the edge of the board with the bit clear of the stock at one end and the guide block flush against the face of the workpiece. As you feed the bit through the cut, keep the base plate flat on the board's edge and the guide block pressed against the workpiece *(above, right)*. Reposition the board, if necessary, to avoid hitting the vise with the clamp.

SHOP TIP

Eliminating tearout
Routers have a tendency to cause tearout, particularly as they exit a workpiece at the end of a dado cut. To minimize splintering, always use an edge guide for straight cuts and secure a wood block the same thickness as your workpiece along the edge from which the bit will emerge. The pressure of the block against the workpiece will help to eliminate tearout.

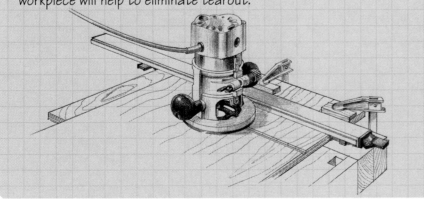

ADJUSTABLE DADO JIG

The jig shown at right is ideal if you do much routing of dadoes in carcase panels. The jig features edge guides to keep the cut perpendicular to the edges of the workpiece and a sliding clamping block to hold the panel securely. Size the pieces so the distance between the edge guides equals the diameter of your router's base plate. The guides should be long enough to allow you to clamp the widest panel you plan to cut.

Cut the four guide pieces, the two ends, and shims from ¾-inch plywood; make all the pieces 4 inches wide. Assemble the end and guide pieces so the router base plate is flush against the guides along their entire length. Then screw the pieces together, sandwiching the end pieces between the guides. At one end of the frame, attach shims to the top and bottom of the end piece. Countersink all your fasteners. Cut

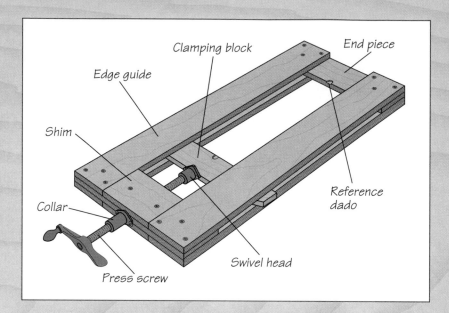

the clamping block from ¾-inch-thick stock; make it about 3 inches wide and long enough to slide between the edge guides. To install the press screw, bore a hole for the threads through the shimmed end piece.

Remove the swivel head from the press screw and fasten it to the middle of the clamping block. Attach the threaded section to the swivel head and screw the collar to the end piece. Use the router to cut short reference dadoes in the other end piece and the clamping block.

To use the jig, slide the workpiece between the edge guides, aligning the cutting lines with the reference dadoes. Secure the panel in position with the press screw. Clamp the jig to a work surface. With the bit clear of the work, turn on the router and start the cut at the reference dado in the end piece, making certain the router is between the edge guides. Feed the bit into the workpiece, keeping the base plate flat on the stock *(left)*. To minimize tearout, only raise the router clear of the work once the bit exits the workpiece and reaches the reference dado in the clamping block.

GROOVING ON A ROUTER TABLE

Mounted upside down in a table, the router works very much like a shaper. In addition to carving decorative contours on board edges and making precise joinery cuts, a table-mounted router offers a safe and quick method to cut dadoes and grooves. The setup allows you to exert greater control over routing operations.

Virtually any dadoing operation can be performed with a table-mounted router, but the arrangement is particularly convenient for cutting grooves in narrow stock *(below)*. Stopped grooves can be cut with either a straight bit or a three-wing slotting cutter. As shown on page 76, your best choice is the slotting cutter since it allows the workpiece to be pivoted into the cutter with the face of the board flat on the

table. With a straight bit, the stock is lowered onto the bit edge down, with the board face resting against the fence—a trickier operation.

Remember that several light cuts are safer and more accurate than one heavy pass. If you need to cut a groove wider than your largest straight bit, make two or more passes, advancing the fence after each pass. For deep grooves, also make a series of cuts, increasing the cutting depth for each pass.

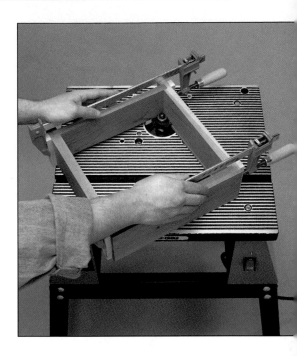

A table-mounted router fitted with a piloted three-wing slotting cutter routs a groove along the inside of a drawer for a bottom panel. Keeping the pilot against the stock keeps the groove depth uniform and controls kickback.

CUTTING A GROOVE IN A BOARD EDGE

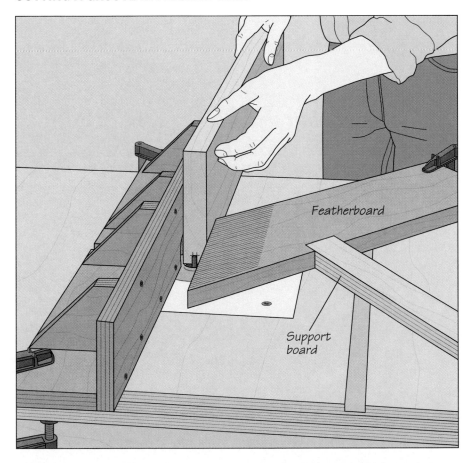

Featherboard

Support board

Making the cut
With a straight bit in the router, set the cutting depth and align the cutting marks with the bit. For the shop-built router table and clamp-on fence shown in the illustration, position the fence flush against the board face and secure it to the tabletop; make certain the fence is parallel to the edge of the table. To secure the workpiece, clamp a featherboard to the table opposite the bit; clamp a support board at a 90° angle to the featherboard for extra pressure. Feed the workpiece into the bit, pressing the stock firmly against the fence *(left)*. If you are working with narrow stock, protect your fingers from the bit using a push stick.

CUTTING A STOPPED GROOVE

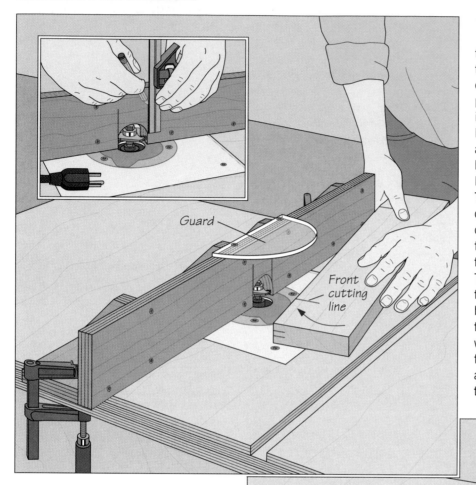

Guard

Front
cutting
line

1 Setting up and starting the cut
Mount your router in a table with a three-wing slotting cutter in the tool. Mark two sets of cutting lines on the workpiece: one on its leading end for the width and position of the groove and the other on its face for the length of the groove. Butt the marks on the end of the board against the cutter and adjust the cutter height. Install the fence on the table, lining it up with the pilot on the cutter. To help you determine the location of the cutter when it is hidden by the workpiece during this cut, mark the points on the fence where the bit starts and stops cutting *(inset)*. Attach the guard to the fence. To start the cut, turn on the router with the workpiece clear of the bit. Hold the board face down on the table and align the front cutting line on the workpiece with the bit cutting mark on the fence farthest from you. Bracing the board against your thigh, slowly pivot it into the cutter *(left)*.

2 Finishing the cut
When the workpiece is flush against the fence, feed it forward while pressing it down and against the fence. Continue the cut until the back cutting line on the workpiece aligns with the bit cutting mark closest to you. Pivot the trailing end of the workpiece away from the cutter with your right hand *(right)*, steadying the board against the table and fence by hooking your left hand around the edge of the table. Avoid lifting the board until the stock is clear of the cutter. Use a chisel to square the ends of the groove, if necessary.

RABBETS

A rabbet is one of the most basic of cuts, commonly used in a corner joint or to accommodate the back of a cabinet. Few tools do the job better or more quickly than a router. As shown below, a rabbet can be routed with a piloted rabbeting bit, although a straight bit in conjunction with an edge guide will work equally well.

With a piloted bit, the pilot bearing rides along the edge of the workpiece while the cutting edges above the bearing rout the stock. The width of the rabbet is equal to one-half the difference between the diameter of the bit and the diameter of the bearing. A 1¼-inch-diameter bit with a ½-inch bearing, for example, will cut a rabbet ⅜ inch wide.

So that woodworkers do not have to own a different bit for each possible rabbet, many router bit manufacturers now sell rabbeting sets, consisting of a single cutter and a selection of different-sized bearings.

A straight bit and an edge guide *(page 78)* can be used to cut rabbets of any width: The cutter can be positioned at any distance from the edge of the stock.

A rabbeting bit carves a stopped rabbet into the underside of a shelf. The rabbet will fit into a wooden shelf support attached to the side of a carcase. This technique conceals both the rabbet and the shelf support.

To rout extra-wide rabbets that exceed the capacity of your largest bit, make two or more passes, adjusting the location of the edge guide each time.

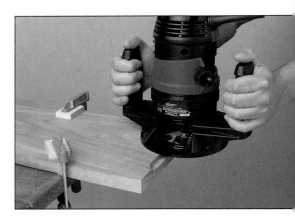

CUTTING A RABBET

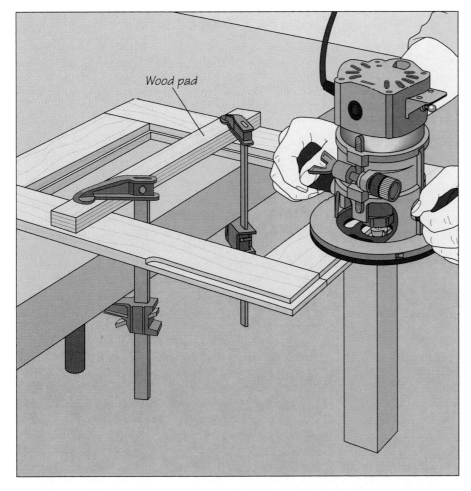

Wood pad

Using a piloted bit

Clamp your stock to a work surface; for the door frame shown, about one-half of the workpiece should extend beyond the table's edge. Gripping the router firmly with both hands, butt its base plate on the workpiece and guide the bit into the stock; make sure the cutting edge is clear of the table. Keeping the pilot bearing pressed against the edge of the workpiece, feed the bit around the perimeter of the frame in a counterclockwise direction *(left)*. Once the bit nears the table on the other side of the workpiece, stop the cut and turn off the router. Loosen the clamps, rotate the workpiece, and clamp it again. Follow the same routing procedures to complete the operation.

BUILD IT YOURSELF

RABBETING JIG

Make it easy to cut wide or non-standard-width rabbets with a straight bit and the simple jig shown at right. Made from two strips of wood, the jig is simple to assemble and set up.

Cut the base from plywood or solid stock the same thickness as your workpiece. Make the edge guide from ¾-inch plywood. Both pieces should be at least as long as the largest piece you plan to cut.

To set up the jig, secure the stock to a work surface and outline the rabbet on it. Butt the jig base against the edge of the stock. Align the bit over the cutting mark, then position the edge guide flush against the router base plate. Fasten the edge guide to the base of the jig with countersunk screws, ensuring that both boards are parallel to the edge of the

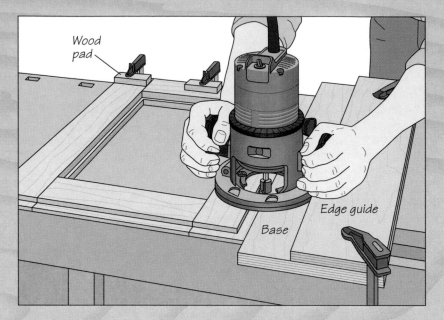

Wood pad

Edge guide

Base

workpiece. Clamp the jig in position. In making the cut, feed the bit against the direction of bit rotation and keep

the tool's base plate pressed firmly against the edge guide throughout the operation.

SHOP TIP

Cutting rabbets of different widths
Instead of stocking several bits of different diameters, you can buy a rabbeting kit, consisting of a single cutter and a set of pilot bearings of various sizes. A typical kit allows you to cut rabbets ranging in width from ¼ to 7/16 inch. Use a hex wrench to install the appropriate bearing for the rabbet you wish to cut. If you already own a piloted rabbeting bit, you can still benefit from this convenience by buying the bearings separately.

CIRCULAR GROOVES

The router is one of the few tools that excel at making both curved and straight cuts with equal ease. Assisted by a guide or jig that maintains the distance between the bit and the center of the circle, the router can cut decorative curves and circles with unerring precision. One of the many styles of commercial guides available is shown in the photo at right, but the circle and edge guide supplied with the router, like that illustrated on page 66, is usually adequate for the task. Rather than pivoting around a fixed point at a circle's center, this guide follows the edge of the workpiece and is useful only when the circular cut is concentric with the circumference of the workpiece.

While commercial jigs can be adjusted to cut circles of varying diameters, some guides are too short to cut larger arcs. A shop-made jig like that described on page 80 will solve this problem.

As with cutting dadoes, a plunge router is more convenient than a standard tool for routing circles. And remember, for safety's sake and to reduce tearout, cut deep grooves with several passes, rather than in one cut.

A router cuts a decorative groove in a tabletop with the help of a commercial circle guide. Fixed to the stock with a screw, the jig pivots around the center of the circle. The screw hole can be concealed later with a wood plug.

ROUTING A CIRCLE

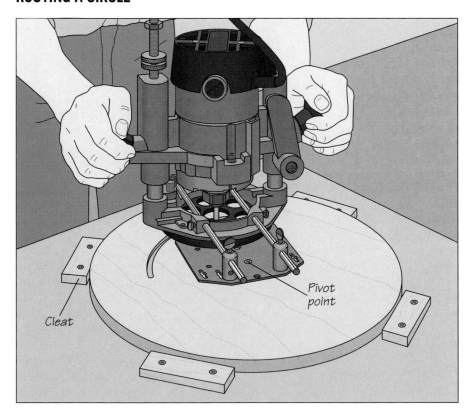

Cleat

Pivot point

Using a plunge router
Butt wood scraps as cleats against the edges of the workpiece and screw them in place. Install a straight bit in the router, then mark the location of the groove and the center of the circle. Use a screw or the fulcrum pin provided with a commercial circle-cutting guide to fix the pivot point of the jig to the center of the circle; the guide should be secure, but able to pivot. Install the router on the guide so the bit is aligned with the groove mark. With the cutter clear of the workpiece, grip the router firmly and plunge the bit into the stock. Feed the tool steadily in a clockwise direction *(left)* until the circle is completed.

BUILD IT YOURSELF

COMPASS JIG

To cut larger circles than most commercial circle-cutting guides allow, use the compass jig shown below. Make the device from ¼-inch hardboard, sizing the jig to suit your router and the radius of the largest circle you plan to cut. Cut the router-end of the jig in the shape of a circle about the size of your tool's base plate. The arm of the jig should be at least 2 inches wide and longer than the radius of the circle you will be cutting. Cut out the jig with a band saw or a saber saw, then bore a hole in the center of the rounded end to accommodate the router bit. To mount the jig on your router, remove the sub-base and set the tool on the circular part of the jig. With the bit centered over the hole, mark the locations of the predrilled holes in the base plate. Bore the holes and screw the jig to the router. Finally, draw a line down the center of the jig arm.

To use the jig, determine the radius of the circle you wish to cut and transfer this length to the jig, measuring from the edge of the bit closest to the center of the circle along the center line. Bore a hole at the center mark, then screw the jig to the workpiece. Secure the stock to a work surface with cleats. Rout the circle as you would with a commercial guide *(page 79)*, guiding the router in a clockwise direction.

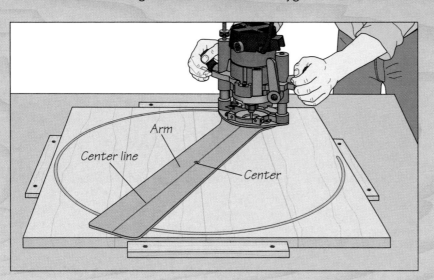

Arm

Center line

Center

SHOP TIP

Quick compass jig
Use a strip of perforated hardboard cut slightly wider than the router base plate to fabricate a simple shop-made circle-cutting jig for your tool. Cut the strip so that one row of holes runs down the center of the jig. Use the jig as described above, but attach it to your router and the workpiece through the hardboard's existing perforations.

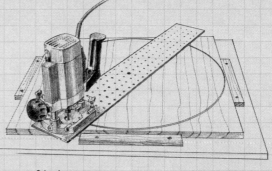

PATTERN GROOVING

Pattern grooving is used not only for cutting decorative grooves, recesses for inlay, and producing multiple copies of the same design, but also for such workaday, but demanding, tasks as cutting hinge-and-lock mortises. The procedure involves fixing a template to the workpiece and using it to guide the router bit.

You can buy templates for some jobs, or you can easily make your own. There are two main methods of pattern grooving: one with the hand-held router and another with the tool mounted in a pin routing attachment.

Mounted in a pin routing attachment, a router cuts a groove in a workpiece front. A template with the desired pattern is fixed to the underside of the workpiece and a guide pin in the table ensures that the pattern is accurately reproduced.

The exact procedure you follow for hand-held pattern routing depends on the type of bit you use. With a top-piloted bit, all you need is a carefully prepared template. Non-piloted bits require a template along with a template guide.

A plunge or pin router is your best choice for grooving the interior of a workpiece, since the bit can be easily and accurately lowered into the stock. Pin routing is examined in detail beginning on page 84.

PATTERN GROOVING WITH A TEMPLATE GUIDE

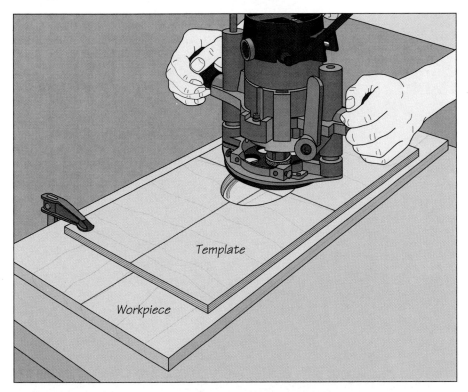

Template

Workpiece

Using a plunge router
Install a template guide on your router and prepare a template of the pattern you wish to reproduce *(page 38)*. Set the stock on a work surface and clamp the template on top of it in the desired position. To make the interior cut shown, set the router flat on the template with the guide butted against the inside edge of the template. Plunge the bit into the stock, then feed the tool in a clockwise direction *(left)*. Complete the cut, keeping the guide in contact with the edge of the template throughout the operation.

Using a standard router

Set up your stock and router as you would for working with a plunge router *(page 81)*. With the tool on the template, tilt it so the bit is clear of the stock, but aligned over the marked outline. Gripping the router firmly, turn it on and lower the cutter into the workpiece until the base plate is flat on the surface and the template guide is butted against the edge of the template *(left)*. Feed the bit in a clockwise direction until the cut is finished; ride the guide along the template throughout the operation.

CUTTING A HINGE MORTISE

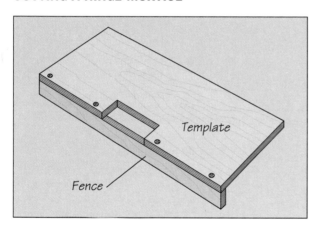

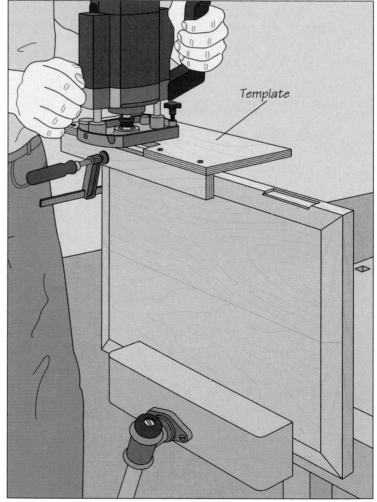

Using a template

Pattern routing is an excellent method for cutting mortises for hinges. Install a straight bit and a template guide in your router. Then make the template from a piece of ¾-inch plywood that is wide enough to support the router. Outline the hinge leaf on the template, being sure to compensate for the template guide and the thickness of the fence, which is also made from ¾-inch plywood. Cut out the template, then attach the fence with countersunk screws *(above)*. To use the jig, secure the door edge up, mark the hinge outline on the workpiece, and clamp the template in position, aligning the cut-out with the outline on the door edge and butting the fence against the face of the door. Make the cut *(right)*, moving the router in small clockwise circles until the bottom of the recess is smooth, then square the corners with a wood chisel.

ADJUSTABLE ROUTING GUIDE

The jig shown at right is ideal for routing rectangular grooves and it can be fitted with templates for curved cuts. The jig can be adjusted to a wide range of sizes and proportions.

Cut the four guides from 1-by-2 stock, making them long enough to accommodate the largest workpiece you plan to handle. The guides are assembled using a combination of grooves, tenons, mortises, and hanger bolts. Rout a continuous groove—⅜ inch deep and wide—along the inside edge of each guide. Then cut a two-shouldered tenon at one end of each guide; size the tenon to fit in the groove. Bore a pilot hole into the middle of each tenon for a ⅜-inch-diameter hanger bolt. Screw the bolts in place, leaving enough thread protruding to feed the bolt through the adjacent edge guide and slip on a washer and wing nut. Finally, rout ⅜-inch-wide mortises

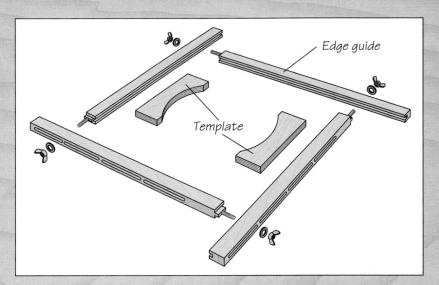

Edge guide

Template

through the guides; starting about 3½ inches from each end, make the cuts 4 inches long, separated by about ½ inch of solid wood. Assemble the jig by slipping the tenons and hanger bolts through the grooves and mortises of the adjacent guide and installing the washers and nuts. To produce a curved pattern, you will also need to make templates like the ones in the illustration to guide the router along the contours; use double-sided tape to secure the templates to the workpiece.

To use the jig, set your stock on a work surface and outline the pattern on the surface. Loosen the wing nuts of the jig, then position it on the stock so the edge guides frame the outline. Place the router flat on the workpiece and align the bit with one edge of the outline. Butt one of the edge guides flush against the router base plate. Repeat on the other edges until all four guides and any templates for curved cuts are in position. Tighten the wing nuts, reposition the jig on the workpiece, and clamp it in place. Plunge the bit into the stock and make the cut in a clockwise direction, keeping the base plate flush against an edge guide or template at all times. For repeat cuts, simply clamp the jig to the new workpiece and rout the pattern (left).

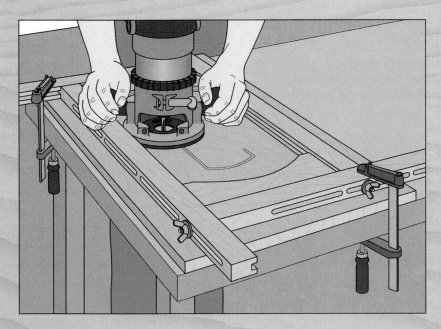

GROOVING WITH A PIN ROUTER

Mounting a router in a pin routing attachment is an especially efficient way of making interior cuts. All you need to carve out a recess or rout a curve is a template with the desired pattern cut into it. The template is fastened to the bottom of the workpiece with double-sided tape or, if the underside of the stock will not be visible, screws. With the router in the attach-

Suspended in a pin routing attachment, a router fitted with a core box bit carves a decorative groove into the stiles of a cabinet door. Feeding the workpiece with its edge flush against the fence ensures a straight cut.

ment, the bit is aligned directly above a guide pin installed on the surface of the work table. Movement of the workpiece and template on the table is determined by the pin, allowing the bit to reproduce the template pattern in the top face of the stock. Resist the temptation to cut grooves with the pin routing attachment freehand—without the guide pin in place—or you may experience kickback. Take the time to build a template and use the pin.

To cut straight grooves with the pin routing attachment, remove the guide pin and install a fence on the table, as shown in the photo at left. Refer to page 58 for details on setting up your pin routing attachment.

CUTTING A RECESS

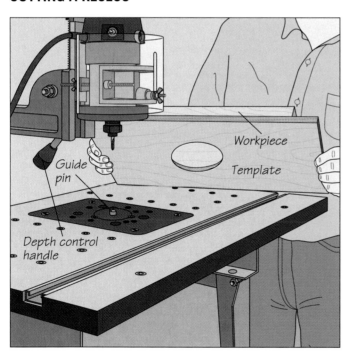

Guide pin

Depth control handle

Workpiece

Template

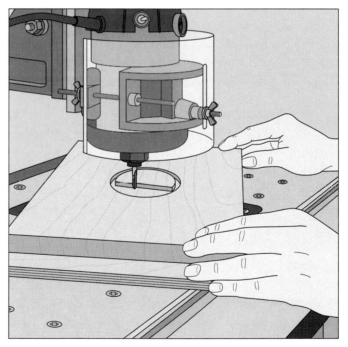

Making the cut

Mount your router in the pin routing attachment and install a guide pin in the table directly below the bit. Make a template with the pattern you wish to produce and fasten it to the underside of the stock. Set the template and workpiece on the table so the guide pin will be within the cut-out *(above, left),* and set the depth of cut. With the bit clear of the stock, turn on the router. Holding the workpiece steady with one hand, pull down on the depth control handle to lower the router and plunge the bit into the stock. Feed the workpiece against the direction of bit rotation, keeping the template flat on the table and the guide pin flush against the edges of the pattern. Once the bit has cut a groove around the rim of the recess, remove the waste progressively *(above, right),* continuing until the bottom of the depression is smooth. **(Caution: Blade guard raised for clarity.)**

CUTTING INTERIOR GROOVES WITH A SHOP-MADE PIN ROUTER

1 **Setting up and starting the cut**
Pin routing provides an accurate way to rout a groove parallel to a curved edge of a workpiece. Build a pin routing jig *(page 63)* and mount your router in a router table. Set the workpiece on the table and align the marks for the width of the groove with the bit. Clamp the jig to the table so the guide pin is in line with the bit and butts against the edge of the workpiece. To start the cut, turn on the router with the stock clear of the bit. Holding the end of the board square to the cutter, advance the workpiece until the edge contacts the guide pin and the bit bites into the stock *(right)*.

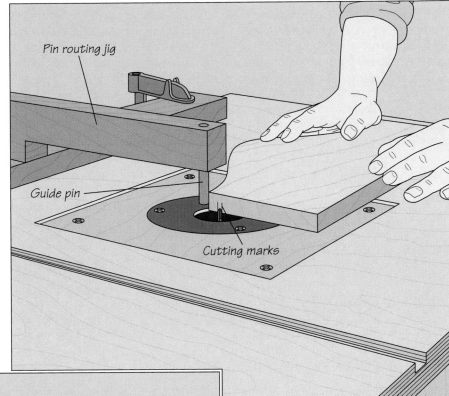

Pin routing jig

Guide pin

Cutting marks

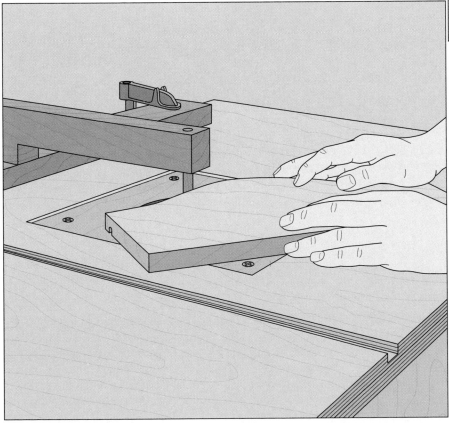

2 **Completing the cut**
Feed the workpiece into the bit, applying lateral pressure to keep the edge of the stock against the guide pin. To ensure that the groove is parallel to the workpiece's curved edge, pivot the stock to keep the portion of the edge being cut parallel to the end of the jig arm at all times *(left)*, making sure your hands are clear of the cutter when the bit exits the workpiece.

INLAYING

Inlaying is the decorative process of setting a thin strip of wood into a recess cut in the surface of a workpiece. A wide range of inlays is available, from simple bands of exotic wood to elaborate marquetry motifs consisting of several veneers assembled into an attractive design. An example of the latter is shown below. Before the development of the router, recesses for inlays used to be cut with a wood chisel or a router plane—a laborious, time-consuming task. A router fitted with a straight bit can complete this chore quickly and precisely. Still, it is an exacting task because the depression must match the inlay precisely. Following the steps presented below and opposite will help you achieve good results. With edge guides to confine the router's movements, you can be assured of a perfect match between the size of the recess and the dimensions of the inlay.

Recesses for marquetry inlay should be as deep or slightly deeper than the thickness of the inlay, typically $\frac{1}{20}$ inch. If the inlay is slightly recessed after the glue has dried, carefully sand the wood surrounding the inlay until the two surfaces are flush. If you are using solid wood inlay—thicker than marquetry—make the recess slightly shallower than the inlay's thickness, and sand the two surfaces even after glue-up. Spread a very thin layer of glue to secure the inlay in place. One final tip: Before plowing the recess, score its outline with a chisel or knife to avoid tearout along the edges.

A marquetry inlay, formed from a pattern of dyed wood set in a veneer, graces a mahogany board. The inlay was glued into a routed recess.

SETTING A MARQUETRY INLAY IN PLACE

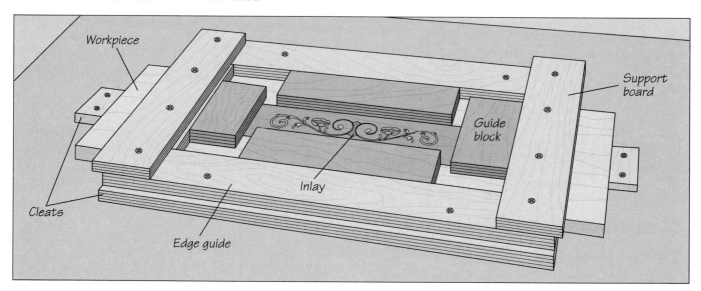

Workpiece

Support board

Guide block

Inlay

Cleats

Edge guide

1 Setting up the edge guides

After you set your stock on a work surface, butt wood scraps against the edges as cleats and screw them in place. Position the inlay and outline its edges on the surface. Then cut a strip of ¾-inch plywood so its width equals the distance between the edge of your router's base plate and its bit. Saw the strip into four pieces and butt them against the edges of the inlay to serve as guide blocks. Then rest four more plywood pieces against the guide blocks as edge guides. To keep the guides from moving, screw them to the cleats; in cases where this would involve screwing directly into the workpiece, such as at the ends of the workpiece shown, fasten support boards to the guides, then screw the boards to the guides that are already fixed in place *(above)*. Remove the inlay and guide blocks. Riding your router base plate against the edge guides ensures the recess will fit the inlay exactly.

2 Routing the recess

Set the router's cutting depth. Make a test cut in a scrap board and test-fit the inlay; adjust the cutting depth, if necessary. To make the cut, rest the router on the workpiece with the bit clear of the stock and above the outline. Then turn on the router and plunge the bit into the workpiece. Guide the tool in a clockwise direction to cut the outside edges of the recess, keeping the base plate flush against an edge guide at all times *(right)*. To complete the recess, rout out the remaining waste, feeding the tool against the direction of bit rotation as much as possible. Use a chisel to square the corners.

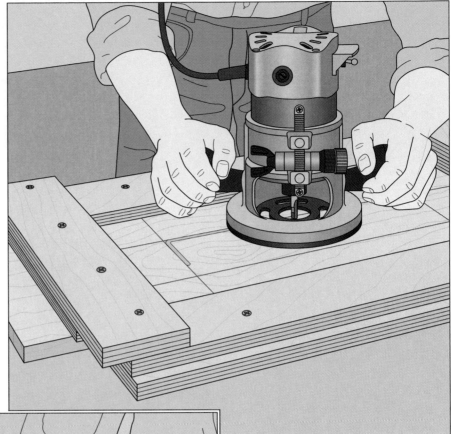

3 Gluing up the inlay

Once the recess is completed, cut a wood pad slightly smaller than the recess to hold the inlay in place. Spread a thin layer of glue in the recess and position the inlay in place, paper-side-up. Lay a piece of wax paper over the inlay to prevent the wood pad from bonding to it. Then set the pad in place. Use as many C clamps as necessary to distribute the clamping pressure evenly. Starting about 1 inch from the ends of the wood pad, space the clamps at 3- to 4-inch intervals; focus the pressure on the top half of the pad. Tighten the clamps just enough to hold the pad in place, then turn the workpiece over so that the first row of clamps is resting on the work surface. Install the second row of clamps along the other edge of the pad *(left)*. Finish tightening all of the clamps firmly.

Wood pad

ROUTER JOINERY

Paired with a multi-joint jig, a router makes quick work of carving the pins of a dovetail joint.

The router's ability to plunge into wood and cut precise, clean, straight-edged grooves makes it an excellent tool for the demanding task of joinery. Equipped with a battery of specially designed bits, jigs, and other accessories, the router can cut dozens of joints, ranging from the utilitarian rabbet to the most elaborate of dovetails. A dozen of these joints is presented on page 90. The remaining pages of the chapter provide step-by-step instructions for fashioning the cuts.

The mortise-and-tenon is the most popular method of assembling the frame in frame-and-panel construction. Many commercial jigs are available to help you cut this joint with a router. Some are essentially positioning jigs for centering the router bit on the edge of a workpiece *(page 93)*. Other models are used to cut the joints for the rails and stiles of a frame *(page 94)*. Shop-built jigs for routing mortises *(page 96)* and tenons *(page 97)* can also be made inexpensively. Another common frame-and-panel joint—the cope-and-stick *(page 98)*—offers strength and a decorative flourish.

Dovetail joints are best cut with the help of a variety of commercial jigs. Whether you cut the half-blind variety *(page 100)*, a common drawer joint, or the traditional through dovetail *(page 101)*, these jigs will help you produce the joint with unerring precision.

Joints can be either functional or decorative—or both. The sliding dovetail *(page 103)* and glue joint *(page 107)*, for example, are strong joints that remain invisible once they are assembled. The dovetail spline *(page 105)*, on the other hand, is primarily a visual detail. The butterfly key joint *(page 112)* fulfills both roles, reinforcing edge-to-edge butt joints while embellishing the surface with its double-wing motif.

Some joints, perhaps because they require long or repetitive cuts, are best produced on the router table. The box joint *(page 108)* and tongue-and-groove *(page 114)* are good examples.

For a seamless fit, a long, interlocking joint like the tongue-and-groove calls for precision cutting. Here, the groove half of the joint is plowed on a router table by a three-wing slotting cutter.

ROUTER-MADE JOINTS

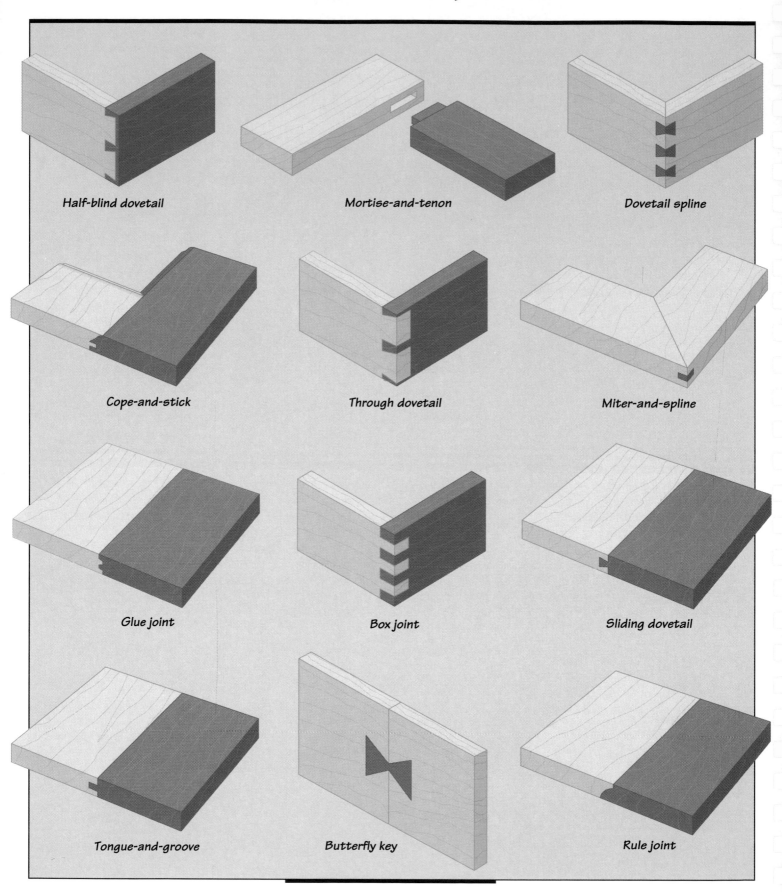

Half-blind dovetail

Mortise-and-tenon

Dovetail spline

Cope-and-stick

Through dovetail

Miter-and-spline

Glue joint

Box joint

Sliding dovetail

Tongue-and-groove

Butterfly key

Rule joint

ROUTER JOINERY JIGS

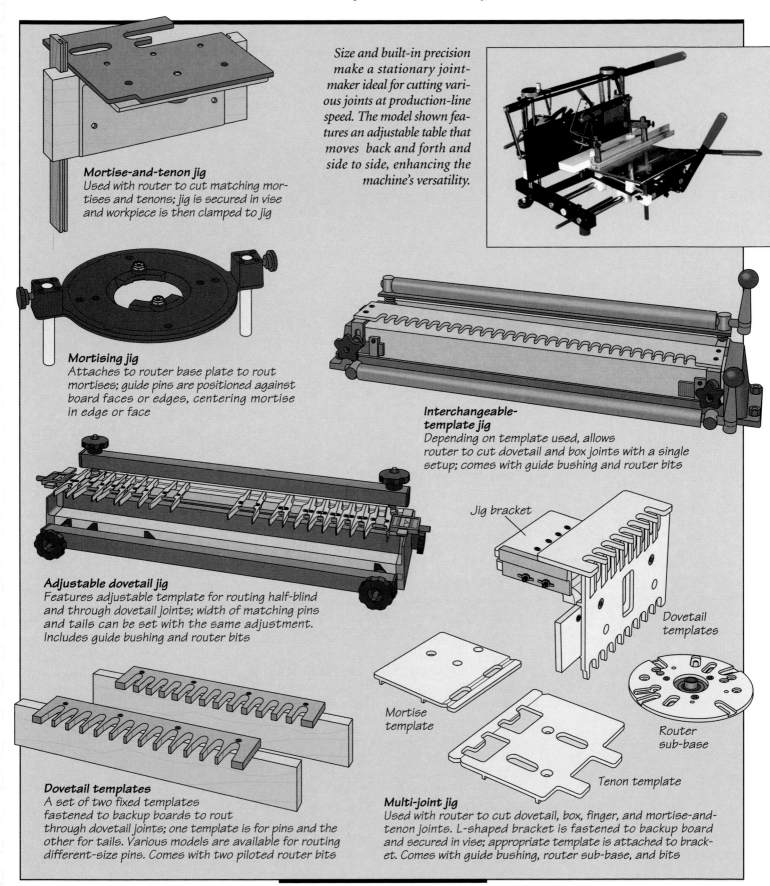

Mortise-and-tenon jig
Used with router to cut matching mortises and tenons; jig is secured in vise and workpiece is then clamped to jig

Size and built-in precision make a stationary joint-maker ideal for cutting various joints at production-line speed. The model shown features an adjustable table that moves back and forth and side to side, enhancing the machine's versatility.

Mortising jig
Attaches to router base plate to rout mortises; guide pins are positioned against board faces or edges, centering mortise in edge or face

Interchangeable-template jig
Depending on template used, allows router to cut dovetail and box joints with a single setup; comes with guide bushing and router bits

Jig bracket

Dovetail templates

Adjustable dovetail jig
Features adjustable template for routing half-blind and through dovetail joints; width of matching pins and tails can be set with the same adjustment. Includes guide bushing and router bits

Mortise template

Router sub-base

Tenon template

Dovetail templates
A set of two fixed templates fastened to backup boards to rout through dovetail joints; one template is for pins and the other for tails. Various models are available for routing different-size pins. Comes with two piloted router bits

Multi-joint jig
Used with router to cut dovetail, box, finger, and mortise-and-tenon joints. L-shaped bracket is fastened to backup board and secured in vise; appropriate template is attached to bracket. Comes with guide bushing, router sub-base, and bits

MORTISE-AND-TENON JOINTS

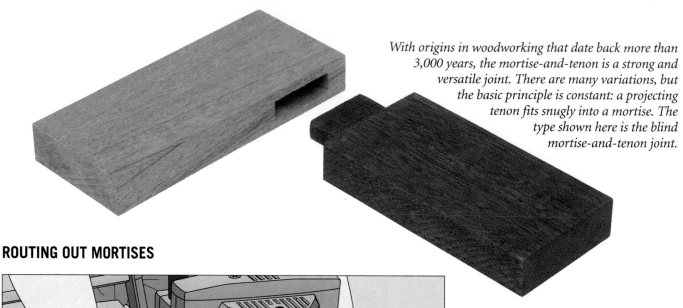

With origins in woodworking that date back more than 3,000 years, the mortise-and-tenon is a strong and versatile joint. There are many variations, but the basic principle is constant: a projecting tenon fits snugly into a mortise. The type shown here is the blind mortise-and-tenon joint.

ROUTING OUT MORTISES

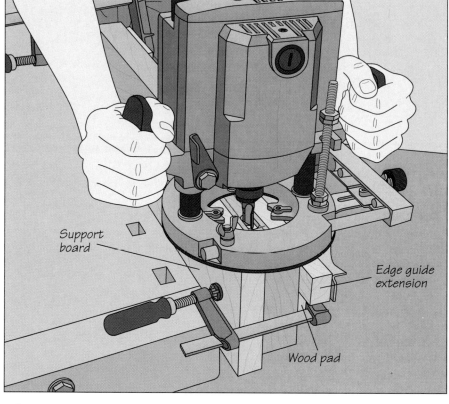

Support board

Edge guide extension

Wood pad

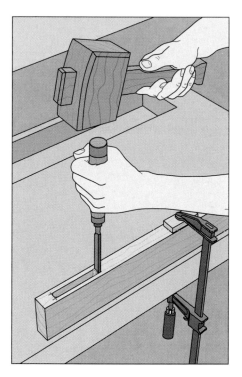

Using an edge guide

Use the tenon, which you can cut with a saw, to outline the mortise on the edge of the workpiece. Then secure the stock edge-up in a vise along with a support board to keep the router steady during the cut; make certain the top surfaces of the two boards are level, and use a wood pad to protect your stock. Install a mortising bit of the same diameter as the width of the mortise, then set the depth of cut. For a deep mortise, make one or more intermediate passes. Attach a wooden extension to the fence of a commercial edge guide, then fasten the guide to the router base plate. Center the bit over the outline and adjust the extension so it rests flush against the workpiece. Holding the router firmly, plunge the bit into the stock at one end of the mortise *(above, left)*, then feed the cutter to the other end. Once the cut is completed, clamp the stock to a work surface and square the corners of the mortise with a chisel *(above, right)*, keeping the blade square to the workpiece and the bevel facing the waste.

Working with a mortising sub-base
Another way to rout mortises is to attach a commercial mortising sub-base to your router's base plate. The jig features two guide pins designed to butt against opposite faces of a workpiece *(inset)*, ensuring that the mortise is centered on the edge. Secure the stock edge-up in a vise and mark the beginning and end of the mortise. Rout the mortise as you would with an edge guide *(page 92)*, making sure the guide pins both ride along the workpiece throughout the cut *(right)*.

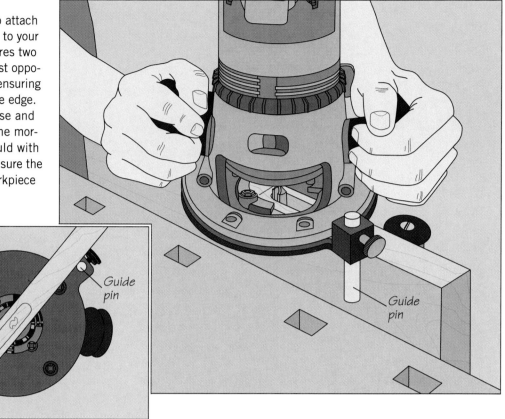

Mortising sub-base

Guide pin

Guide pin

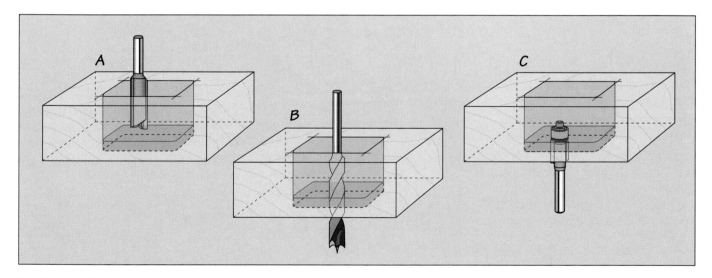

A

B

C

Routing deep through mortises
With the aid of an electric drill, your router can make mortises that exceed its maximum depth of cut. The illustration above shows the three steps necessary to cut a mortise through a thick workpiece. Start by installing a mortising bit in the router and making as many passes as you can until you can go no deeper (A). Then use the drill with a bit bigger than your router bit to bore a hole through the remaining waste (B). Install a piloted flush-trimming bit in the router and turn the workpiece over. Inserting the bit through the hole made by the drill, rout out the waste (C); keep the pilot bearing pressed against the walls of the cavity to complete the mortise.

ROUTING A MORTISE-AND-TENON

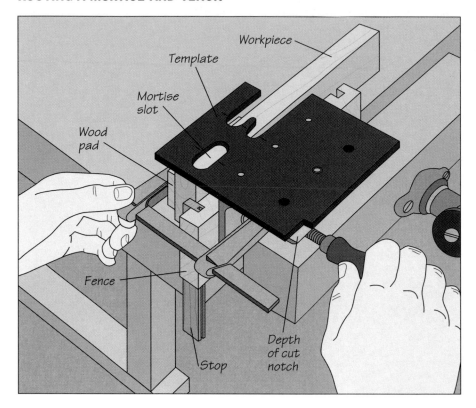

Workpiece

Template

Mortise slot

Wood pad

Fence

Stop

Depth of cut notch

1 Setting up the jig
Assemble a commercial mortise-and-tenon jig following the manufacturer's instructions. The model shown allows you to rout both the mortise and tenon. Secure the jig in a vise, then clamp the workpiece to it, butting the end of the board against the stop and the edge to be mortised against the template. Use wood pads to protect the stock *(left)*. Install the piloted bit supplied with the jig in your router. Use the jig's depth-of-cut notch as an aid to setting the router bit's cutting depth.

2 Routing the mortise
If you are using a plunge router, hold the router flat on the jig template with the bit centered over one end of the mortise slot. Turn on the tool and plunge the bit into the stock *(right)*. With a standard router, you will need to angle the tool and slowly lower the bit into the workpiece. In either case, feed the tool along the template to the other end of the slot to finish the cut, pressing the bit pilot against the inside edge of the slot throughout the cut. Keep the cutting edge from touching the template at any time. Unclamp the stock from the jig and remove the jig from the vise.

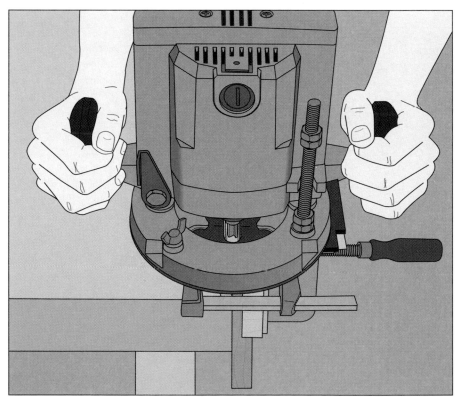

3 Adjusting the jig for the tenon

Remove the jig stop from the fence and fit it in the fence slot at the opposite end of the jig. Unscrew the template from the jig body and shift the template toward the tenon-end slots so that one of the alignment pins on the jig body is exposed. Refasten the template. Secure the jig and the tenon workpiece in the vise, positioning the stock so that its edge butts against the stop and its end is flush against the template *(right)*.

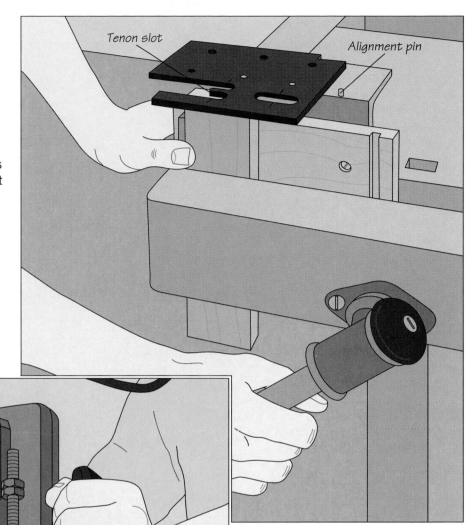

Tenon slot

Alignment pin

4 Routing the tenon

Cut the tenon in two steps. One end of the tenon is cut the same way you routed the mortise in step 2, guiding the bit pilot along the inside edges of the tenon slots *(left)*. Then, without moving the workpiece, unscrew the template from the jig body and turn it end-for-end, keeping the same alignment pin exposed as for the first pass. Finish routing the tenon.

BUILD IT YOURSELF

A MORTISING JIG

The jig at right allows you to rout a mortise in stock of any thickness. Its adjustable jaws ensure that the mortise will be positioned properly, normally centered in the edge of the board.

Cut the jig top from ¾-inch plywood; make the piece about 15 inches long and wide enough to accept the thickest stock you expect to mortise. Cut the two jaws from 2-by-4-inch stock, sawing the pieces to the same length as the top. To prepare the top, mark a line down its center, then cut a notch along the line at one end using a router. The notch should be as wide as the template guide you will use with your router bit. (If you are using a top-piloted bit, rather than a non-piloted straight bit with a template guide, size the notch to accommodate the bearing.) The notch should be long enough to accommodate the longest mortise you expect to cut. Next, rout two adjustment slots perpendicular to the centerline. Finally, bore a viewing hole between the two slots. To assemble the jig, screw hanger bolts into the jaws, then fasten the top to the jaws with washers and wing nuts.

To use the jig, outline the mortise on the workpiece and mark a line down its center. Loosen the wing nuts and secure the stock between the jaws so the centerline is aligned with the line on the jig top; make sure the top edge of the workpiece is butted up against the top. Tighten the wing nuts. Align the bit with one end of the outline, then mark reference lines on the jig top along the edge of the router base plate. Repeat

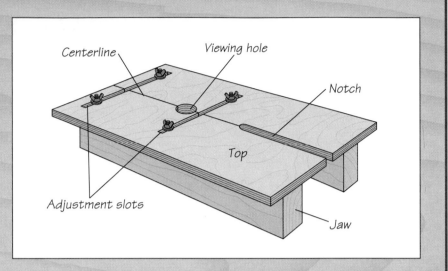

to mark lines at the other end of the outline. Rout the mortise *(below)*, starting the cut with the base plate aligned with the first set of reference lines and stopping it when the plate reaches the second set.

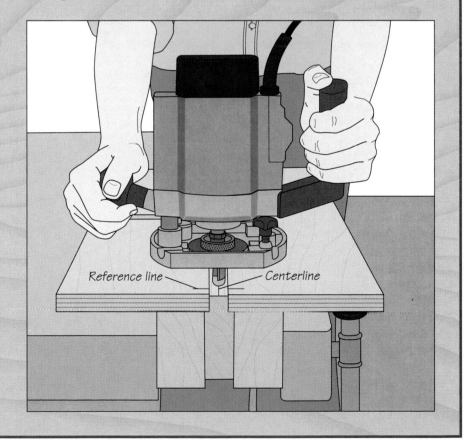

A TENONING JIG

Made of solid wood and plywood, the jig shown at right allows your router to cut square, two-shouldered tenons. The stock sits face-down under the jig while the router rides along a fence on top, removing waste in two passes.

The jig consists of two parallel base pieces, an end stop, and a fence —all made of wood the same thickness as the workpiece, in this case 1-by-3 stock—and a top and support made of ½-inch plywood.

The base pieces should be about 16 inches long; cut the plywood top about 8 by 10 inches and screw it to the base strips as shown at right. Screw the end stop in place underneath the support, and attach the ends of the support to the base strips. Fix the fence about 1 inch from the end of the top.

Countersink all screw heads and be sure to make all angles square. Bore a viewing hole through the top to help you position the workpiece against the base.

You will also need to construct an acrylic sub-base for your router. It should be at least as wide as your router's base and long enough to extend from the fence beyond the end stop; a 10- or 12-inch-square piece will serve well.

Install a ¾-inch bit in the router, then remove the standard sub-base from the tool and use it as a template to mark the screw holes and bit clearance hole in the acrylic sub-base. The new sub-base must be attached to the router so that the edge of the bit lines up with the inner edge of the support and end stop when it rides along the fence. Bore the holes and attach the sub-base to the router.

To use the jig, butt the end of your workpiece against the end stop and the edge flush against the base. Clamp the assembly in place. Set the router's cutting depth and rout out the waste for half the tenon, riding the sub-base along the fence throughout the cut. (You will rout reference dadoes into the base pieces at the same time.) Turn the workpiece over and repeat the cut to complete the tenon (*below, bottom*).

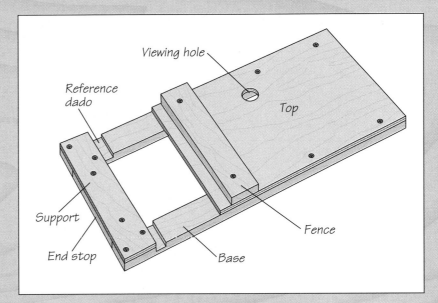

Viewing hole

Reference dado

Top

Support

End stop

Base

Fence

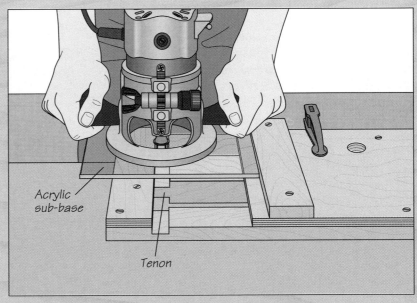

Acrylic sub-base

Tenon

COPE-AND-STICK JOINTS

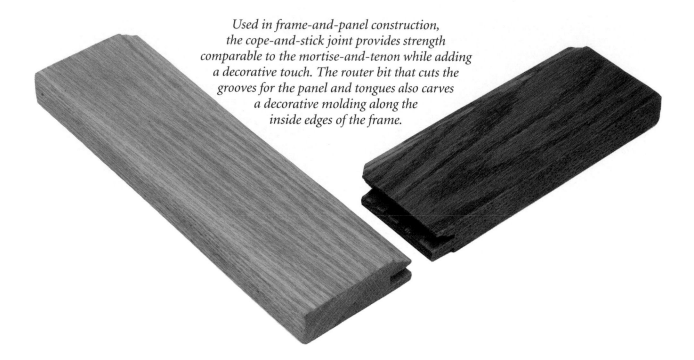

*Used in frame-and-panel construction,
the cope-and-stick joint provides strength
comparable to the mortise-and-tenon while adding
a decorative touch. The router bit that cuts the
grooves for the panel and tongues also carves
a decorative molding along the
inside edges of the frame.*

ROUTING A COPE-AND-STICK JOINT ON THE ROUTER TABLE

1 Cutting the tongues in the rails
Make a cope-and-stick joint by first cutting tongues in the ends of both rails. Then rout grooves for the panel along the inside edges of all four frame pieces; the grooves in the stiles will accommodate the rail tongues at the same time. To cut the tongues, install a piloted coping bit—or rail cutter—in your router and mount the tool in a table. Set the cutting depth by butting the end of a rail against the bit and adjusting the router's depth setting so that the top of the uppermost cutter is slightly above the workpiece. Position the fence parallel to the miter gauge slot and in line with the edge of the bit pilot. Fit the miter gauge with an extension and press the outside face of the stock flat on the table; keep the ends of the workpiece and extension butted against the fence throughout each cut *(right)*.

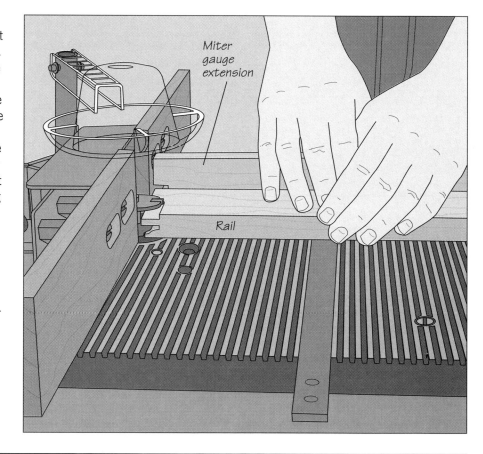

Miter gauge extension

Rail

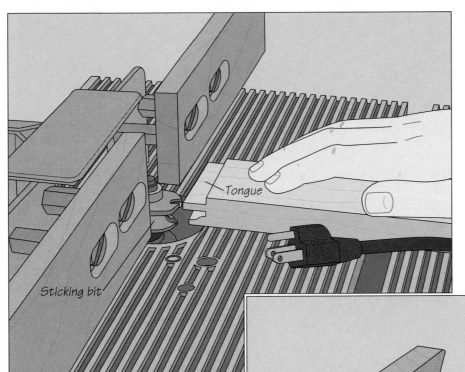

2 Adjusting the sticking bit

Replace the coping bit with a piloted sticking bit—also known as a stile cutter. To set the cutting depth, butt the end of a completed rail against the bit, and raise or lower the bit until one of the groove-cutting teeth is level with the rail tongue *(left)*. Align the fence with the edge of the bit pilot.

3 Cutting the grooves

Use three featherboards to secure the workpiece during the cut. Clamp one to the router table opposite the bit, securing a support board at a 90° angle to the jig. Clamp the other two featherboards to the fence on either side of the cutter. (In this illustration, the featherboard on the outfeed side of the fence has been removed for clarity.) Make each cut with the stock outside-face down, pressing the workpiece against the fence *(right)*. Use a push stick to complete the pass. Repeat this groove cut on all the rails and stiles.

DOVETAIL JOINTS

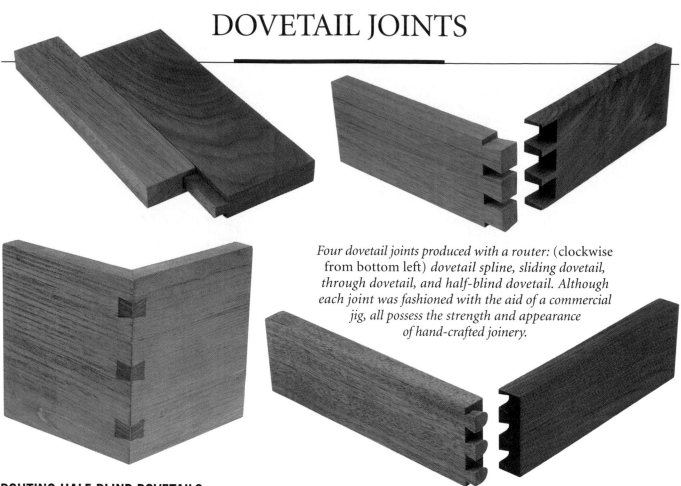

Four dovetail joints produced with a router: (clockwise from bottom left) *dovetail spline, sliding dovetail, through dovetail, and half-blind dovetail. Although each joint was fashioned with the aid of a commercial jig, all possess the strength and appearance of hand-crafted joinery.*

ROUTING HALF-BLIND DOVETAILS

Using an interchangeable-template jig

Set up a commercial jig for half-blind dovetails following the manufacturer's instructions. On the model shown, this involves clamping the pin and tail boards in position against the body of the jig, and securing the appropriate template atop the workpieces. Install the proper bit and template guide on your router, then rout the pins and tails in two passes: Start from the right-hand edge and make a light cut along the edge of the tail board. This will reduce tearout and ensure that all the waste around the tails will be removed. Then make a second full pass starting at the left-hand end of the workpieces, following the contours of the router's template and moving in and out of the slots *(right)*; keep the template guide flush against the edges of the fingers at all times. This will cut the pins and complete the tails simultaneously.

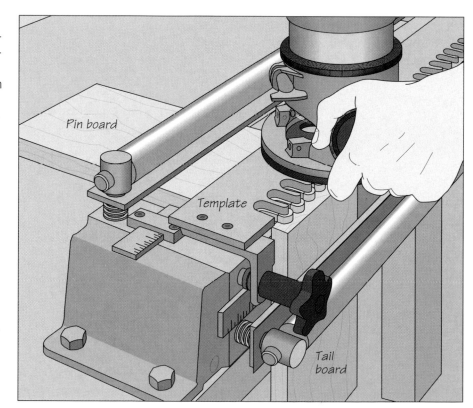

TWO JIGS FOR ROUTING THROUGH DOVETAILS

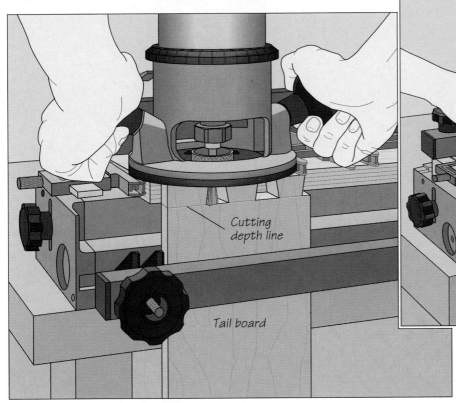

Cutting
depth line

Tail board

Finger
assembly

Spacer board

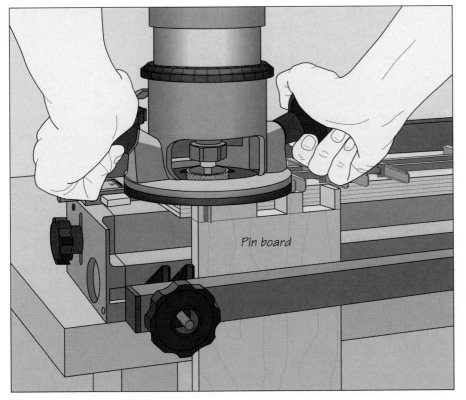

Pin board

Using an adjustable dovetail jig

The jig shown on this page features an adjustable finger assembly that allows you to set the size of the pins and tails you rout as well as the space between them. Adjusting the assembly for the tails automatically gives you the proper size and spacing of the pins. Install a dovetail bit in your router, then set up the jig following the manufacturer's instructions: Clamp a spacer board of ¾-inch plywood to the top of the jig body, and secure the tail board outside-face out. Once the fingers are laid out over the tail board according to the size and spacing you want *(inset)*, use the thickness of the pin board as a guide to mark a cutting depth line across the tail board. Flip over the finger assembly and set the depth of cut on the router to cut the tails *(left, top)*. Rout from right to left, keeping the base plate flat on the fingers. To cut the pins, remove the tail board and turn over the finger assembly. Install a straight bit in the router and clamp the pin board to the jig. Mark a cutting depth line on the board, set the router's depth adjustment, and rout the pins *(left, bottom)*.

Using dovetail templates

To rout through dovetails with the dovetail templates shown on this page, attach the pin and tail templates to backup boards following the manufacturer's instructions. Secure the tail board in a vise end-up and clamp the backup board to it, making sure there will be half-tails at both edges; the template and backup board should be flush against the workpiece. Protect the stock with a wood pad. If you are cutting several workpieces, butt a stop block against the first workpiece and clamp the block to the backup board. Install the dovetail bit and template guide supplied with the jig and cut the tails, feeding the tool in and out of the template slots *(right)*. Unclamp the tail board from the vise and use it to outline the pins on the pin board. Secure the pin board in the vise and clamp the pin template to the stock, aligning the jig fingers with the marked outline. Remove the dovetail bit from the router, install the straight bit supplied with the jig, and rout out the waste between the pins *(below)*.

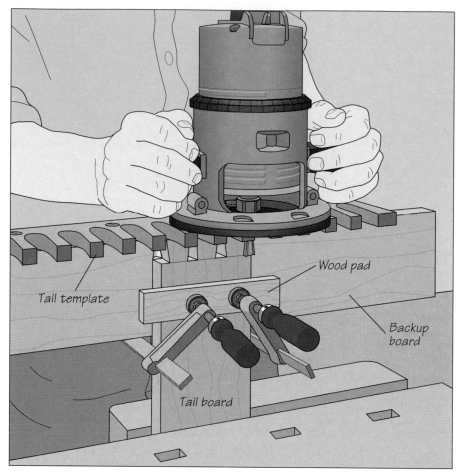

Wood pad

Tail template

Backup board

Tail board

Pin template

Pin board

MAKING A SLIDING DOVETAIL JOINT

1 Cutting the dovetail groove

Cut the dovetail groove in two passes on a router table: Start with a straight bit to remove most of the waste; complete the groove with a dovetail bit. For the first pass, install a straight bit. Adjust the depth of cut, and position the fence so that the work is centered over the bit. Clamp a featherboard to the table to secure the workpiece during the cut; to apply extra pressure, clamp a support board at a 90° angle to the featherboard. Feed the workpiece into the bit with both hands *(right)*, pressing the stock flat against the fence throughout the cut. Finish the cut with a push stick. For the second pass, install a dovetail bit *(inset)* and complete the groove by feeding the workpiece into the bit while pressing the stock tightly against the fence.

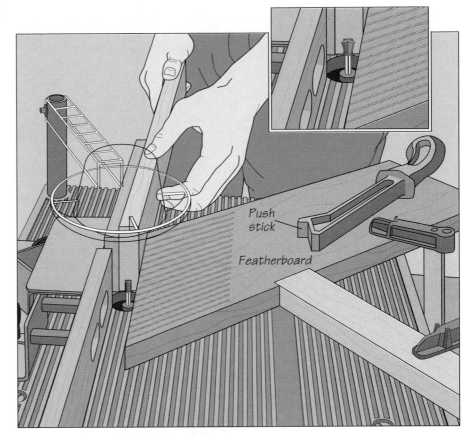

Push stick

Featherboard

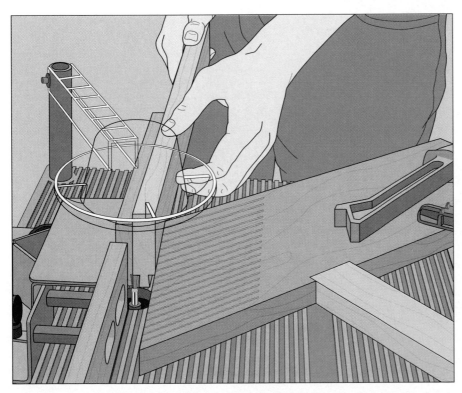

2 Cutting the dovetail slide

With the dovetail bit still in the router, shift the fence toward the bit so that half the diameter of the cutter projects beyond the fence. Reposition the featherboard. Reduce the cutting depth slightly so that the slide is not as deep as the groove; this will improve the fit of the joint. Cut the slide in two passes, removing the waste from one side at a time *(left)*. Test-fit the joint and readjust the position of the fence if it is necessary to trim the slide.

A JIG FOR SLIDING DOVETAILS

The jig shown below allows you to rout sliding dovetails without a router table. The device features a fence that holds the router and a pivoting adjustable table for aligning the workpiece with the bit. Cut the fence, table, and support piece from ¾-inch plywood. Make all the boards 16 inches long; the fence and table should be about 10 inches wide and the support piece about 3 inches wide. Screw the table to the support piece so they form an L shape. Position the table 4 inches from the top of the fence and bore two holes through the fence into the table support. With a straight bit in a router, lengthen the hole on the outfeed side of the fence into a curved slot. Fasten the adjustable end of the table support to the fence with a carriage bolt, washer, and a wing nut. Bolt the infeed side just loose enough for the table to be able to pivot when the other end is raised or lowered.

To prepare the fence for your router, remove the sub-base and use it as a template to mark the screw holes and bit clearance hole on the fence. The bottom edge of the clearance hole should line up with the top of the jig table when the table is level; in the illustration at left, the table is in the lowest position.

To use the jig, secure the fence in a vise and rout the dovetail groove first, then the matching slide. For the groove, install a bit in the router, attach the tool to the jig fence, and adjust the cutting depth. Set the workpiece face-down on the table, butting its edge against the bit. Loosen the wing nut and adjust the table to center the bit on the edge of the stock, then tighten the nut. Secure the workpiece with three featherboards: Clamp one to the table in line with the bit and the other two to the fence on both sides of the cutter. (In the illustration, the featherboard on the outfeed side of the fence has been removed for clarity.) Rout the groove as you would on a router table, using first a straight bit, then a dovetail bit *(page 103)*. To cut the slide, set your workpiece on the table and lower the table to produce a ⅛-inch-wide cut. Make a pass on each side, finishing the cut with a push stick *(left, bottom)*. Test-fit the joint; if necessary, raise the table slightly and make another pass on each side of the stock.

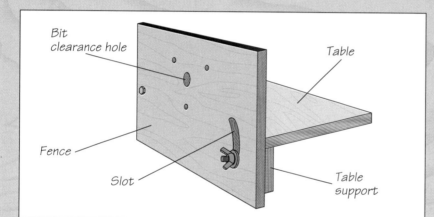

Bit clearance hole

Table

Fence

Slot

Table support

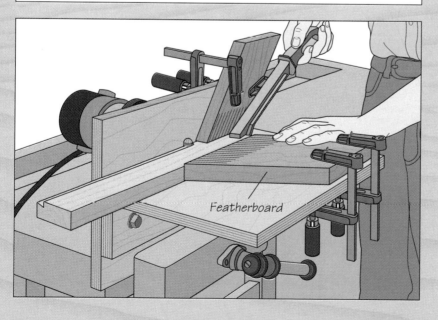

Featherboard

ROUTING A DOVETAIL SPLINE JOINT

1 Making the jig
The jig shown at right, built from ¾-inch plywood, will help you cut grooves for dovetail spline joints in the corners of a carcase. Refer to the illustration for suggested dimensions. Before assembling the jig, cut the oval slot in the middle of the base to accommodate your bit. Cut 45° bevels at the top ends of the arms and the bottom ends of the support brackets. Attach the arms to the base and the brackets to the base and arms, making the arms perpendicular to each other and centering them under the slot. Install a dovetail bit in your router, secure the jig in a vise and, with the bit in the slot, position the edge guide against the tool's base plate and screw it down. Then, with the base plate pressed against the guide, rout a channel across the top ends of the arms.

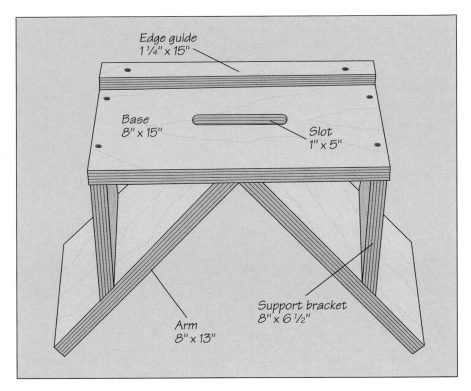

Edge guide
1 ¼" x 15"

Base
8" x 15"

Slot
1" x 5"

Support bracket
8" x 6 ½"

Arm
8" x 13"

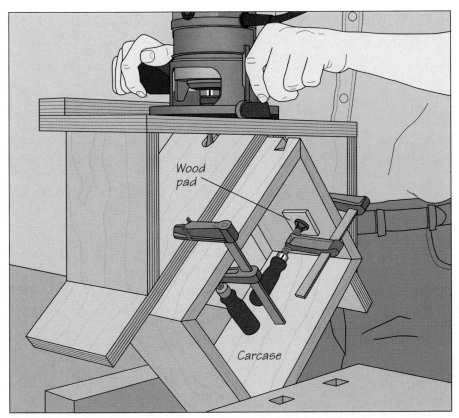

Wood pad

Carcase

2 Routing the grooves
Mark cutting lines for the grooves on the corners of the workpiece. Secure the carcase diagonally in a vise and set the jig on top, aligning the edges of the channel you routed in step 1 with one of the cutting marks. Clamp the jig to the carcase, protecting the stock with wood pads. Rout the grooves by repeating the cut you made to rout the channel, feeding the bit through the corner of the carcase. Be sure to keep the router flat on the jig base and flush against the edge guide until the bit is well clear of the carcase. Reposition the jig and repeat to rout the other grooves *(left)*.

3 Inserting the splines

To make enough splines for several grooves, rout a dovetail slide on the edge of a board, just as you would for a sliding dovetail joint *(page 103)*. Rip the slide from the board on a table saw, then cut individual splines from it. For a snug fit, use the same dovetail bit that cut the grooves in step 2. Install the splines by spreading some glue in the grooves and on the splines and sliding them in place *(right)*. Once the glue has dried, trim off excess wood with a handsaw and sand the surface flush with the carcase.

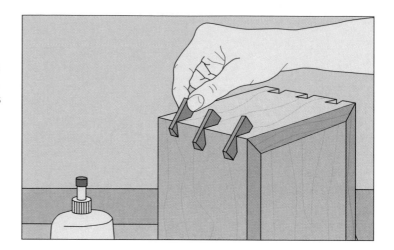

A ROUTER-TABLE JIG

The jig shown below allows you to rout a series of evenly spaced grooves for straight or dovetail splines. Cut a V-shaped notch into the face of a board, then install a ¼-inch straight bit in your router and mount the tool in a table. Screw the jig to a miter gauge and feed it into the bit to make a notch. Fit and glue a wood key in the notch, then reposition the jig on the gauge so the distance between the key and the bit equals the spac-ing you want between the spline grooves. Feed the jig into the bit to rout a second notch. Install a ½-inch dovetail bit and set the depth of cut so the full dovetail shape is visible above the bottom of the notch.

To use the jig, seat the workpiece in the V with an edge butted against the key and rout the first groove. To cut subsequent grooves, fit the groove over the key and slide the workpiece into the bit *(below)*.

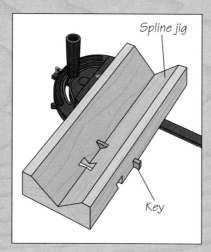

Spline jig

Key

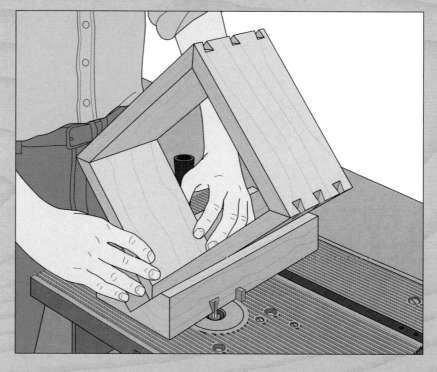

GLUE JOINTS

Used to reinforce glued-up panels, the glue joint consists of two boards with identical cuts in their edges. Both cuts are produced on a router table with the same bit; one of the boards is flipped to mate with the other.

CUTTING A GLUE JOINT ON A ROUTER TABLE

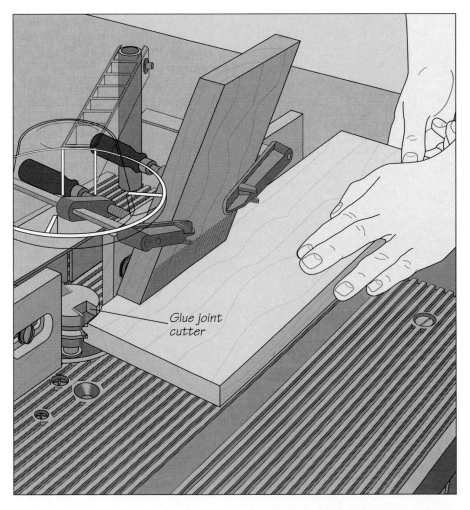

Glue joint cutter

Making the cuts

Install a glue joint cutter in your router, mount the tool in a table and set the cutting depth. Secure the workpiece with two featherboards clamped to the fence on either side of the bit. (In the illustration, the featherboard on the outfeed side of the fence has been removed for clarity.) Before you cut the joint, make test cuts in two scrap boards. Flip one board over, test-fit the joint and, if necessary, adjust the depth of cut until the mated surfaces of the two boards are flush. To make a pass, feed the stock into the bit with your right hand while keeping it pressed firmly against the fence with your left hand *(left)*.

BOX JOINTS

The box joint, also known as a finger joint, is ideal for making drawers or cabinets. The joint derives its strength from the large gluing area of the interlocking pins and notches.

ROUTING A BOX JOINT

1 Setting up the jig

The jig shown at right allows you to cut the notches for a box joint one at a time on a router table. The jig is simply an extension board screwed to the miter gauge and fitted with a key to determine the spacing of the notches. Install a straight bit with the same diameter as the desired width of the notches; mount the router in a table. Set the depth of cut to equal the thickness of your stock and feed the extension into the bit to rout a notch. Then unscrew the extension from the miter gauge and reposition it so that the gap between the notch and the bit equals the width of the bit. Feed the extension into the bit again, cutting a second notch *(right)*. Fashion a wood key to fit in the first notch and glue it in place so it projects about 1 inch from the extension board.

Miter gauge extension

2 Cutting the notches in the first board

Holding the face of the workpiece against the miter gauge extension, butt one edge against the key. Turn on the router and, hooking your thumbs around the gauge, slide the board into the bit, cutting the first notch *(right)*. Fit the notch over the key and make a second cut. Continue cutting notches this way until you reach the opposite edge of the workpiece.

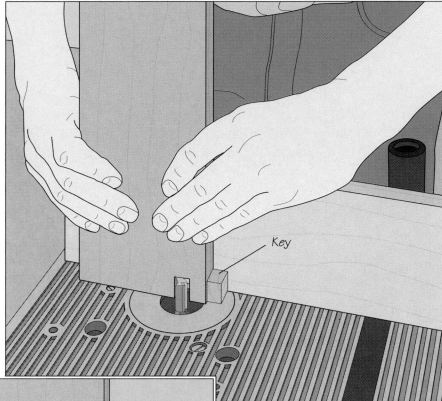

Key

Mating board

3 Cutting the notches in the mating board

Fit the last notch of the first board over the key. Butt one edge of the mating board against the first board, and move the entire assembly forward to cut the first notch in the mating board; hold both pieces flush against the miter gauge extension *(left)*. Cut the remaining notches in the mating board by following the same procedure used for the first board.

MITER-AND-SPLINE JOINTS

The miter-and-spline is essentially a simple miter joint with a spline glued into grooves cut in mitered ends; it is often used in frame-and-panel construction. The spline is either plywood, or solid wood with grain that runs perpendicular to the miter cuts.

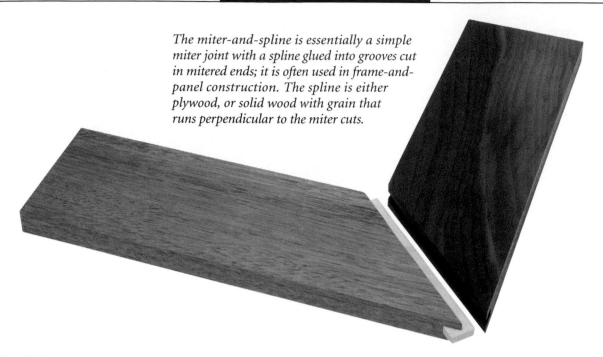

TWO WAYS OF ROUTING A MITER-AND-SPLINE JOINT

Using a straight bit

Make 45° miter cuts in each workpiece. Install a straight bit in your router and mount the tool in a table. Set the cutting depth so the groove you cut will accommodate one-half the width of your spline. To secure the workpiece, clamp a featherboard to the table in line with the bit. Rest the featherboard on a shim so the stock will be held flat against the fence; clamp a support board at a 90° angle to the featherboard to apply extra pressure. Rout the spline grooves by feeding the workpiece on end into the bit, keeping its face flush against the fence *(right)*. Once all the grooves have been made, cut a spline for each joint; make it twice as wide as the groove depth, less 1/32 inch for clearance. For maximum strength, use plywood or solid wood with the grain running across the width of the spline, rather than lengthwise.

Support board

Shim

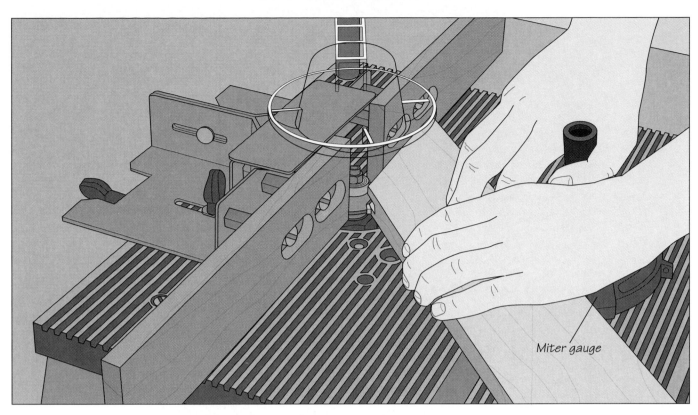

Miter gauge

Using a three-wing slotting cutter
You can also rout the grooves for miter-and-spline joints by using a three-wing slotting cutter and feeding the stock face-down into the bit. Position the fence in line with the bit pilot, making the cutting width equal to one-half the bit diameter. To set the depth of cut, place the workpiece flat on the table and center the bit's tooth on the edge of the stock. Feed the workpiece into the cutter with a miter gauge, holding the edge of the board flush against the gauge and one mitered end flat along the fence (*above*).

SHOP TIP

A miter-and-spline jig
To rout the groove for a miter-and-spline joint along a board edge, use the jig shown here. Cut a 4-by-4 longer than your workpiece, then rip it diagonally. In one piece, joint the cut surface and rout a groove down its middle, then glue a spline in the groove to serve as an edge guide. To use the jig, cut a 45° bevel along the edge of the workpiece, then clamp the stock and the jig to a table with the edge of the workpiece slightly overhanging the jig. Use the router fitted with a straight bit to trim the beveled edge, then install a three-wing slotting cutter and repeat to rout the groove, keeping the bit pilot against the stock.

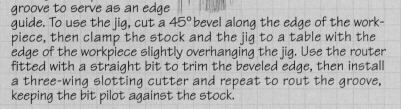

BUTTERFLY KEY JOINTS

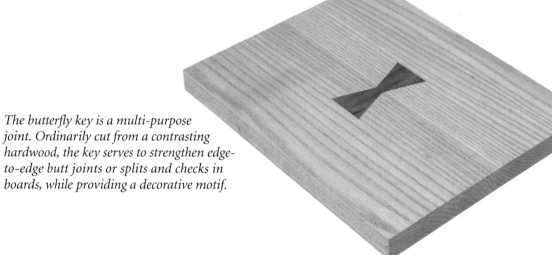

The butterfly key is a multi-purpose joint. Ordinarily cut from a contrasting hardwood, the key serves to strengthen edge-to-edge butt joints or splits and checks in boards, while providing a decorative motif.

MAKING A BUTTERFLY KEY JOINT

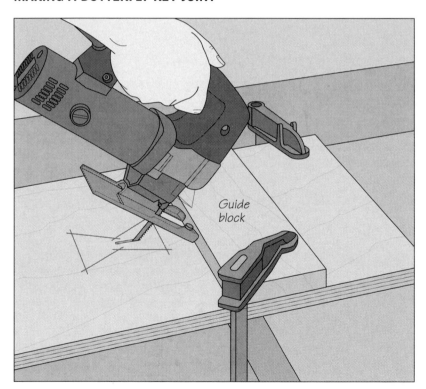

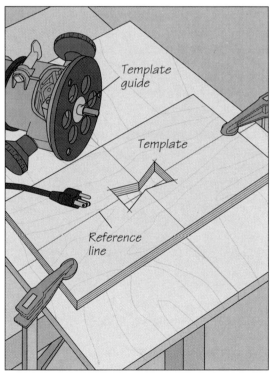

1 Routing the recess

Rout the recess for a butterfly key using a router guided by a template. To make the template, draw the pattern of the key on a piece of plywood that is smaller than your panel. Use a saber saw to cut out the pattern: Clamp a guide block to the template and plunge the saw blade into the stock within the outline while keeping the tool's base plate butted against the block *(above, left)*. Turn off the saw, remove the block and cut out the waste. Carefully sand the edges of the pattern since the router will transfer any imperfections from the template to the recess. Mark intersecting reference lines for the location of each key on the workpiece and template. Then clamp the template atop the stock, aligning the reference lines *(above, right)*. Install a straight bit and template guide in the router; set the depth of cut to no more than one-half the thickness of the workpiece. Rout out the recess, riding the template guide along the edges of the pattern throughout the operation. Square the corners of the recess with a chisel.

2 Cutting the key

Clamp your template atop a hardwood board; the stock should be at least 1/4 inch thicker than the depth of the recess you routed in step 1. Set the cutting depth on the router for a 1/16-inch-deep cut, then make a light scoring cut around the template. Cut out the key on the band saw, aligning the blade with the outside edge of the scored recess *(right)*. Keep your hands clear of the blade as you make the cuts.

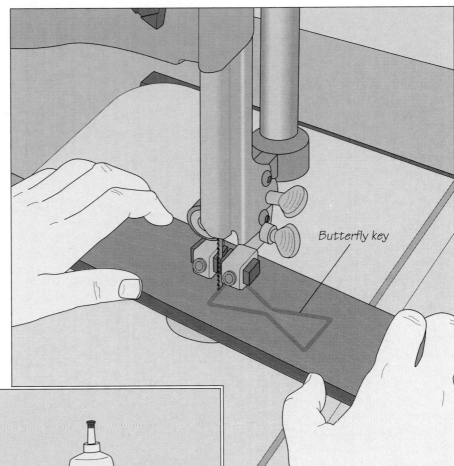

Butterfly key

Wood pad

3 Gluing the key in the panel

Test-fit the key in the recess. If necessary, use a chisel to trim its edges. Once you are satisfied with the fit, spread glue in the recess and insert the key. To focus the clamping pressure, lay a wood pad across the workpiece and clamp both ends *(left)*. Tighten each clamp a little at a time until a thin glue bead squeezes out from under the key. Once the glue has dried, gently sand the surface to trim the key flush with the surrounding wood.

TONGUE-AND-GROOVE JOINTS

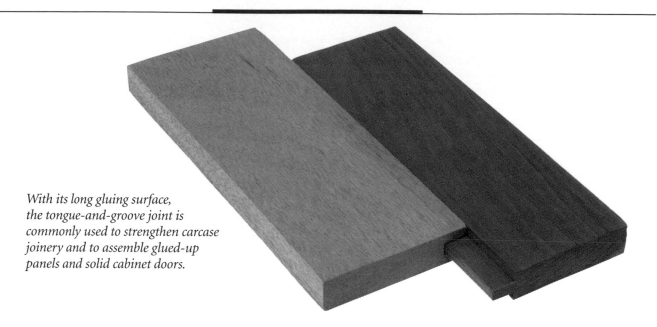

With its long gluing surface, the tongue-and-groove joint is commonly used to strengthen carcase joinery and to assemble glued-up panels and solid cabinet doors.

CUTTING A TONGUE-AND-GROOVE JOINT

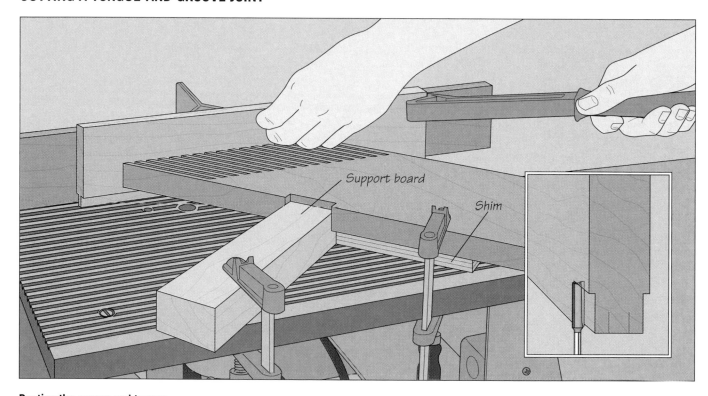

Support board

Shim

Routing the groove and tongue

Fit your router with a straight bit. Start by cutting the groove *(page 75)*, then cut the tongue in several passes, removing the waste a little at a time *(inset)*. The tongue's depth should be slightly less than the groove. To support the workpiece during the cut, clamp a featherboard to the table and rest it on a shim so that it presses against the workpiece above the bit; clamp a sup-port board at a 90° angle to the featherboard for extra pressure. Slowly feed the stock into the cutter. Turn the workpiece end-for-end and repeat the procedure. Finish each pass with a push stick *(above)*. Move the fence back from the bit to remove more waste and make two more passes, test-fitting the joint and continuing until the tongue fits snugly in the groove.

RULE JOINTS

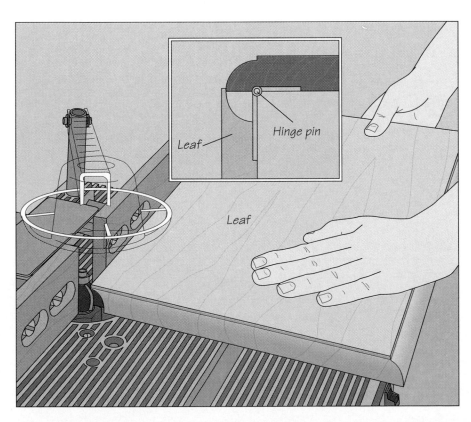

A common feature of drop-leaf tables, the rule joint consists of two matching hinged pieces. The leaf has a cove cut along its edge that mates with the tabletop's rounded-over edge. When the leaf is down, the decorative edge is visible.

MAKING A RULE JOINT

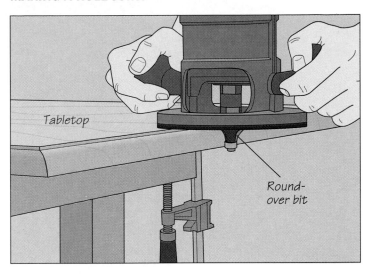

1 Making the cut in the tabletop
Clamp the tabletop to a work surface with the edge to be shaped extending off the surface. Install a piloted round-over bit and adjust the cutting depth to allow you to reach the final depth in at least two passes. As you make the cut, press the bit pilot against the stock throughout the pass *(above)*. For a smooth finish, make your final pass a slow and shallow one.

2 Shaping the leaf and installing the hinge
Install a piloted cove bit whose diameter and profile match the one used in step 1, then mount the router in a table. Align the fence with the bit pilot so that the width of cut will equal one-half the cutter diameter. Set the depth of cut to reach your final depth in several passes. Feed the leaf into the bit, bracing its edge against the fence *(left)*. After each pass, test-fit the pieces; continue cutting until the tabletop and leaf mesh with a slight gap between the two. Finish the joint by installing a rule-joint hinge on the undersides of the pieces: Position one hinge leaf against the tabletop and the other against the leaf so the hinge pin is aligned with the start of the round-over cut on the tabletop *(inset)*. Outline and then rout mortises for the hinge leaves in the tabletop and the leaf. Screw the hinge in place.

SHAPER

The shaper is a common sight in production shops, where it is unequaled for constructing cabinet doors. The panel-raising jig shown above allows arched top rails and arched raised panels to be shaped quickly, safely, and accurately.

The shaper and the router share a common heritage. In the mid-19th Century an inventor in Ohio produced a prototype for a machine with a vertical spindle projecting out of a horizontal table. This machine, known as a spindle router, was virtually identical to the present-day shaper. Another model from the same era, employing an overhead spindle to raise panels and cut grooves and recesses, evolved into today's router.

Similar origins notwithstanding, the router and shaper have since followed different paths. The router is often considered the most useful and versatile woodworking power tool; the shaper, on the other hand, is frequently the last machine added to the woodworking shop, a fact that belies its usefulness to the craftsman.

If you frequently cut decorative moldings in the edges of curved workpieces, or if you build many doors and drawers, the shaper is an ideal tool for your shop. Basically, the machine is a bigger, stronger, and more stable version of a table-mounted router, with a much wider range of available cutters. Shaper cutters *(pages 120)* vary from simple, single profile cutters to complex combination systems that produce the contours of a host of individual blades. Relatively safe and easy to work with, solid cutters with carbide teeth are the preferred choice, though many woodworkers still opt for the versatility of grinding their own knives to whatever profile they desire.

With its large cutter exposed above the table, the shaper requires special attention to safety; the tool is often considered to be the most dangerous machine in the shop. Key concerns are the rotation of the spindle, the direction of feed, and the location of the cutter with regard to the workpiece. Most shaper spindles and cutters are designed to rotate either clockwise or counterclockwise; each direction offers its own advantages and disadvantages. Most cutters are designed to cut from above a workpiece while spinning counterclockwise (as seen from above). This offers a better view of the cut and, because of the direction of the threads on the spindle, ensures that the nut securing the cutter in place remains tight throughout the operation. By reversing spindle rotation and inverting the cutter so that it lies mostly below table level, you can shape the underside of the workpiece. This is often a safer setup for freehand shaping or for working with extra-wide or very long stock. If the workpiece lifts up, the cutter will not gouge it and kick the board back.

Read your owner's manual carefully and follow the setup and cutting guidelines discussed here, starting on page 123. Take the time to build the guards and fence shown on pages 126 and 127; they will make your machine much safer to use.

With a workpiece secured on a template with toggle clamps, a straight cutter cuts a curve with ease and precision. The resulting edge is smoother than could be produced on a band saw; using a template ensures perfect copies of the original pattern.

ANATOMY OF A SHAPER

The shaper works very much like a table-mounted router, but it is larger, heavier, and generally more powerful. The heart of the machine is its spindle, a threaded ½- to 1¼-inch-diameter assembly that typically turns a cutter from 7,000 to 10,000 rpm. The spindle, in turn, is driven by a belt- or direct-drive mechanism connected to a ½- to 5-horsepower motor. Some models offer variable speeds.

Shapers are sized by spindle diameter. Machines with larger-diameter spindles require more powerful motors, but these tools vibrate less, produce cleaner cuts and can be used with a wider assortment of cutters. Many shapers feature interchangeable spindles.

Shaper cutters and accessories are secured to the spindle with a nut and lock washer. The spindle normally turns counterclockwise. On many machines, spindle rotation can be reversed by flicking a switch located on the motor junction box. This is a valuable feature, allowing stock to be fed from either side of the table.

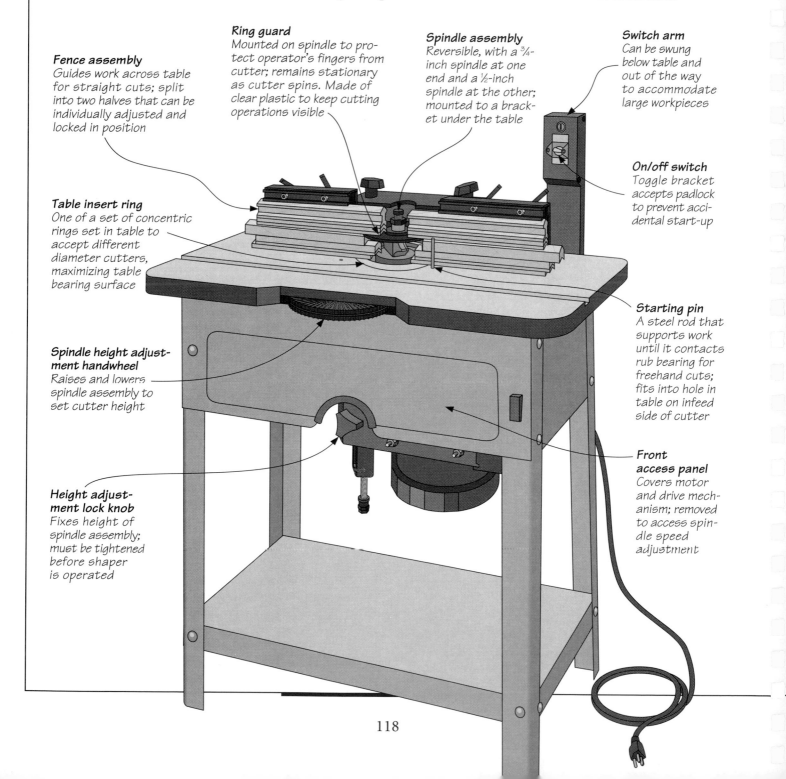

Ring guard
Mounted on spindle to protect operator's fingers from cutter; remains stationary as cutter spins. Made of clear plastic to keep cutting operations visible

Spindle assembly
Reversible, with a ¾-inch spindle at one end and a ½-inch spindle at the other; mounted to a bracket under the table

Switch arm
Can be swung below table and out of the way to accommodate large workpieces

Fence assembly
Guides work across table for straight cuts; split into two halves that can be individually adjusted and locked in position

On/off switch
Toggle bracket accepts padlock to prevent accidental start-up

Table insert ring
One of a set of concentric rings set in table to accept different diameter cutters, maximizing table bearing surface

Spindle height adjustment handwheel
Raises and lowers spindle assembly to set cutter height

Starting pin
A steel rod that supports work until it contacts rub bearing for freehand cuts; fits into hole in table on infeed side of cutter

Height adjustment lock knob
Fixes height of spindle assembly; must be tightened before shaper is operated

Front access panel
Covers motor and drive mechanism; removed to access spindle speed adjustment

Depending on the model, the height of the spindle can be adjusted from 2 to 6 inches.

Few cuts on the shaper are made without an accessory or a jig. Most shaper tables feature a miter gauge slot. Straight cuts should be guided by the fence or a miter gauge. While some fences are comprised of two solid arms that can be moved close to the cutters, the type of fence shown below has segments that slide laterally to conform more closely to the cutter shape, providing an extra measure of safety. Curved work can be shaped with a jig, or a template or starting pin used in conjunction with a rub bearing, which must be mounted on the spindle.

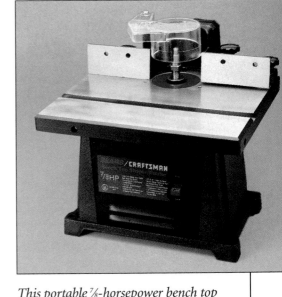

This portable ⅞-horsepower bench top shaper can perform most of the functions of a larger tool. It is equipped with a ½-inch spindle and an accessory router chuck, and can turn cutters and router bits at 9,000 rpm.

Fence locking handle
Attached to fence locking rod; tightened to secure fence in position on table to width of cut

Fence segment locking handle
Locks fence segments at desired setting

Fence adjustment knob
Turned to advance or retract fence

Dust chute
For dust collection system

Fence bracket

Fence segments
Individual wooden fingers adjust to frame cutter and ring guard, increasing fence bearing surface and protecting operator's fingers

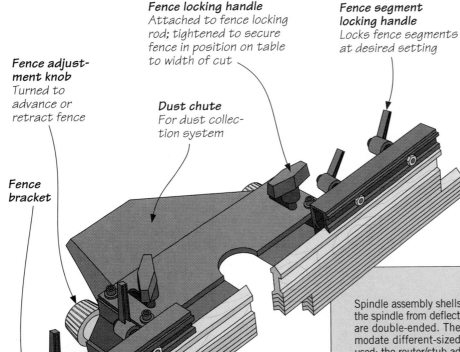

SHAPER SPINDLES

Spindle assembly shells contain two sets of ball bearings that prevent the spindle from deflecting during a cut. Both assemblies shown below are double-ended. The standard assembly *(below, top)* can accommodate different-sized shaper cutters, depending on which end is used; the router/stub adapter assembly *(below, bottom)* accepts router bits at one end and ½-inch-bore cutters at the other.

Spindle assembly

½-inch-diameter spindle

¾-inch-diameter spindle

Spindle shell

Router/stub adapter spindle assembly

Router collet

Stub spindle

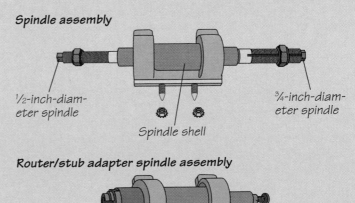

Cutter sets provide a precise method of making snug-fitting joints for frame-and-panel construction. The cut produced by this sticking cutter will mate with the profile carved by its coping counterpart.

Carving decorative molding with a shaper used to involve grinding steel knives to the desired profile in the shop. The knives were then inserted into slotted cutterheads and held in place by friction—an arrangement notorious for releasing the cutters, often with disastrous results.

Today, the knives are ground commercially and normally secured to the cutterhead with hex bolts. (In fact, you should avoid using an assembled cutterhead on a shaper unless it features a method of fixing the knives in place.)

Most knives are made from high-speed steel (HSS) and are available in a variety of profiles. If you have a profile in mind that you cannot find in a catalog and are unable to grind in your own shop, check with a manufacturer of cutters. Some companies will grind knives to your specifications, although the cost can prove prohibitive for the occasional woodworker.

More often, two- and three-wing solid shaper cutters are used by woodworkers. These are usually HSS cutters, tipped with tungsten carbide to provide

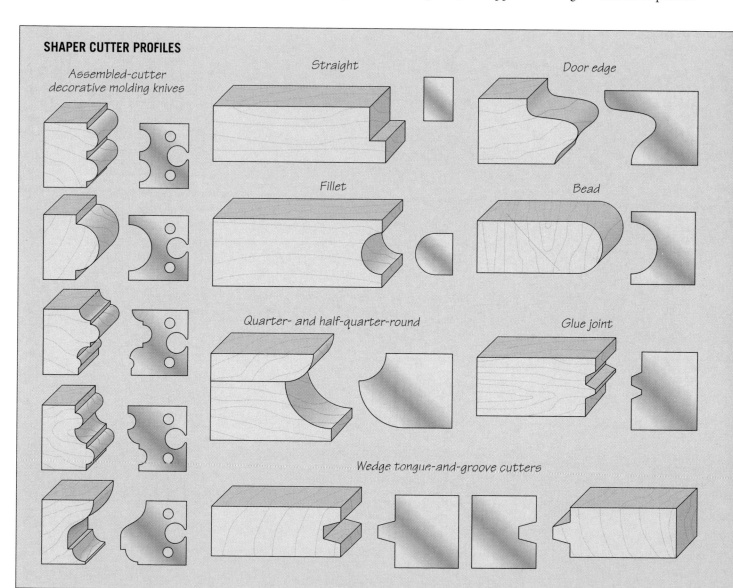

SHAPER CUTTER PROFILES

Assembled-cutter decorative molding knives

Straight

Door edge

Fillet

Bead

Quarter- and half-quarter-round

Glue joint

Wedge tongue-and-groove cutters

a more durable cutting edge. Most solid cutters are sold in standard bore sizes from ½ to 1¼ inches. As shown below, they come in a variety of profiles, from standard detail cutters used for molding to cutter sets like cope-and-stick assemblies, designed to cut both parts of a frame-and-panel joint. Other types, like glue joint and drawer lock cutters, create interlocking profiles for solid joinery. Combination cutters consist of a set of individual blades that produce different profiles depending on how they are stacked on the spindle.

Any shaper cutter will create a different profile according to the thickness of the workpiece and the height of the cutter on the spindle. Make several test cuts before shaping a workpiece. For combination systems and cutter sets, follow the manufacturer's instructions.

You should also refer to the manufacturer's specifications for the required spindle size and maximum rpm rating for a cutter. And although you can use bushings to fit large-bore cutters on small-diameter spindles, the added stress may cause the spindle to deflect.

The quality of your shaper work depends to a great extent on the cutters. Never use a damaged or rusted cutter. Keep cutting edges sharp and wipe them clean after each use. Carbide cutters can be chipped easily, so take care when storing them.

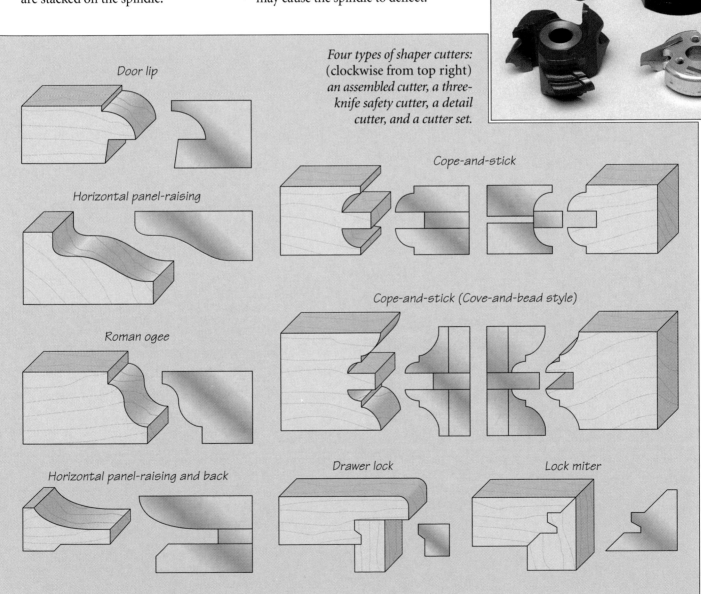

Four types of shaper cutters: (clockwise from top right) an assembled cutter, a three-knife safety cutter, a detail cutter, and a cutter set.

Door lip

Cope-and-stick

Horizontal panel-raising

Cope-and-stick (Cove-and-bead style)

Roman ogee

Horizontal panel-raising and back

Drawer lock

Lock miter

SHAPER ACCESSORIES

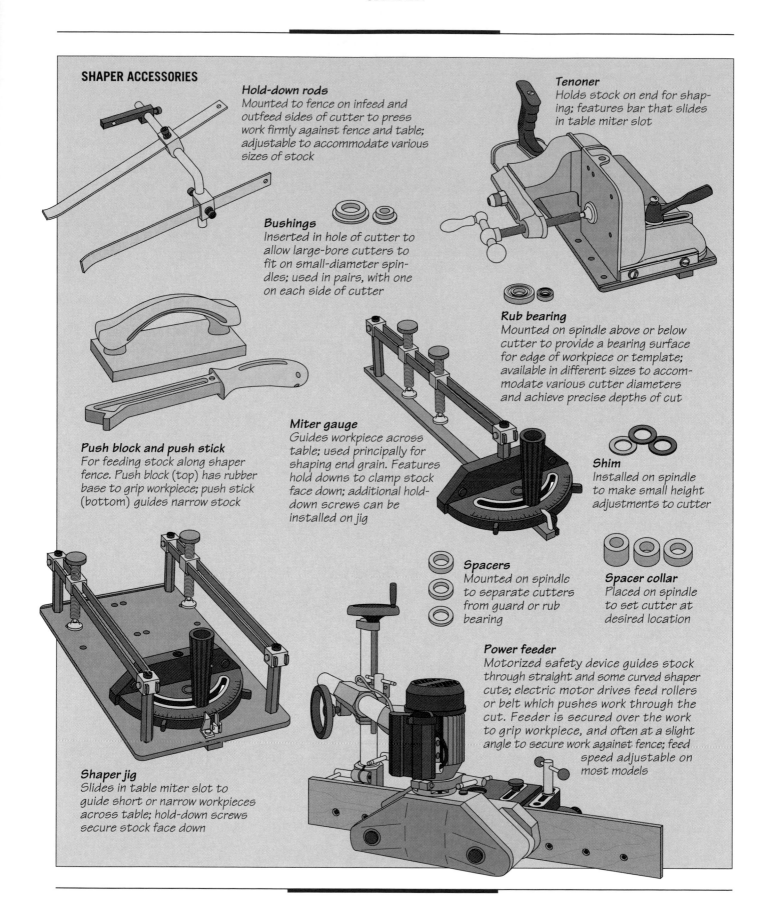

Hold-down rods
Mounted to fence on infeed and outfeed sides of cutter to press work firmly against fence and table; adjustable to accommodate various sizes of stock

Bushings
Inserted in hole of cutter to allow large-bore cutters to fit on small-diameter spindles; used in pairs, with one on each side of cutter

Push block and push stick
For feeding stock along shaper fence. Push block (top) has rubber base to grip workpiece; push stick (bottom) guides narrow stock

Miter gauge
Guides workpiece across table; used principally for shaping end grain. Features hold downs to clamp stock face down; additional hold-down screws can be installed on jig

Tenoner
Holds stock on end for shaping; features bar that slides in table miter slot

Rub bearing
Mounted on spindle above or below cutter to provide a bearing surface for edge of workpiece or template; available in different sizes to accommodate various cutter diameters and achieve precise depths of cut

Shim
Installed on spindle to make small height adjustments to cutter

Spacers
Mounted on spindle to separate cutters from guard or rub bearing

Spacer collar
Placed on spindle to set cutter at desired location

Shaper jig
Slides in table miter slot to guide short or narrow workpieces across table; hold-down screws secure stock face down

Power feeder
Motorized safety device guides stock through straight and some curved shaper cuts; electric motor drives feed rollers or belt which pushes work through the cut. Feeder is secured over the work to grip workpiece, and often at a slight angle to secure work against fence; feed speed adjustable on most models

SETUP AND SAFETY

Few woodworking machines require as much attention to safety as the shaper. Its reputation as a dangerous tool is well-earned: the shaper's high-speed cutters are difficult to guard fully and they are prone to kickback.

Before beginning any shaping operation, make sure the spindle is fastened securely to the machine and its height is locked. Turn the spindle by hand to make sure the cutter turns with the spindle. Any spindle vibration or vertical or lateral motion during a cut can spell trouble. Replace the spindle bearings or the entire assembly if you notice any problems. Periodically perform the test shown below to ensure the spindle shaft turns true.

Two designs for shop-made cutter guards are shown on page 126. When guiding stock along the fence, use a hold-down device. Resist the temptation to shape curves freehand using only the starting pin. Take the time to build a template.

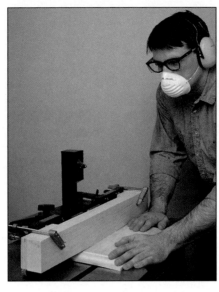

Personal safety gear, such as safety glasses, dust mask, and hearing protection, should be worn for all shaping operations. In addition, the extra-wide featherboard clamped to the fence for this cut helps prevent kickback by keeping the workpiece flat on the table.

CHECKING THE SPINDLE

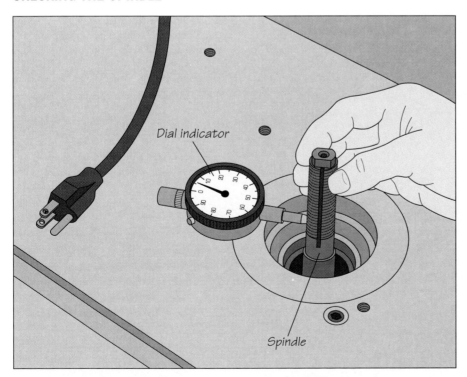

Testing for runout
Set a magnetic-base dial indicator face up on the shaper table so the plunger of the device contacts the spindle. Calibrate the gauge to zero according to the manufacturer's instructions. Then turn the spindle slowly by hand *(left)*. The dial indicator will register spindle runout—the amount of wobble that the spindle would transmit to a cutter. Perform the test at intervals along the length of the spindle, adjusting its height by ½ inch each time. If the runout exceeds 0.005 inch for any of the tests, replace the spindle.

CHANGING A CUTTER

1 Tightening the cutter on the spindle
Insert the appropriate insert ring in the table to support the workpiece. Slide a spacer collar on the spindle so the cutter assembly will sit near the bottom of the shaft, while allowing for a sufficient range of height adjustment. For a freehand cut, mount a rub bearing next. Then slide on the cutter and ring guard. You may need to place a spacer collar on both sides of the cutter to ensure the rub bearing and guard spin freely on the spindle; the cutter should be as close to the bearing as possible without touching it. Slip on another spacer collar, then add the lock washer and nut. Tighten the nut using the two wrenches supplied with the shaper. Hold the spindle steady with one wrench and tighten with the other. For extra leverage, position the wrenches so that you can squeeze them together *(right)*.

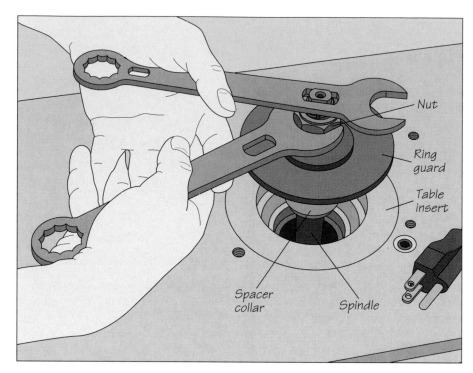

Nut

Ring guard

Table insert

Spacer collar

Spindle

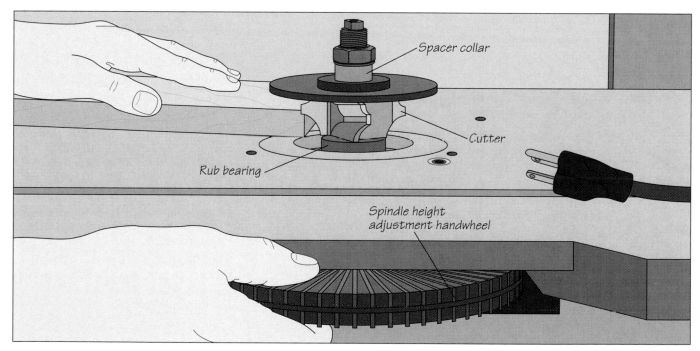

Spacer collar

Cutter

Rub bearing

Spindle height adjustment handwheel

2 Setting the cutter height
Once the cutter has been installed, butt the workpiece against the cutter. Turn the spindle height adjustment handwheel to set the cutting edges to the appropriate height *(above)*: Clockwise raises the spindle; counterclockwise lowers it. To eliminate any play from the handwheel, turn it counterclockwise slightly, then clockwise to the correct setting. Fix the spindle height with the height adjustment lock knob. Make a test cut in a scrap board and readjust the cutter height, if necessary.

SETTING UP THE FENCE

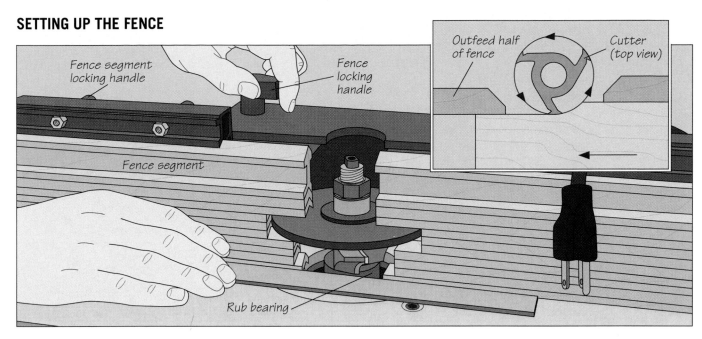

Outfeed half of fence

Cutter (top view)

Fence segment locking handle

Fence locking handle

Fence segment

Rub bearing

1 Adjusting the fence

For the model shown, loosen the four fence segment locking handles and move the wooden segments on both halves of the fence as close as possible to the spindle without touching the cutting edges or guard. Lock the handles, then set the width of cut, moving the fence back from the cutter for a wide pass and advancing it for a shallow cut. For a partial cut, where only a portion of the edge of the workpiece will be removed, loosen the fence lock-

ing handles. Then hold a straightedge against the fence and move both halves as a unit until the straightedge contacts the rub bearing *(above)*. Tighten the handles. If you are making a full cut, in which the cutter will shape the entire edge of the workpiece, turn off the shaper a few inches into the cut. Holding the board in place against the fence, advance the outfeed half until it butts against the cut part of the stock *(inset)*, then finish the pass.

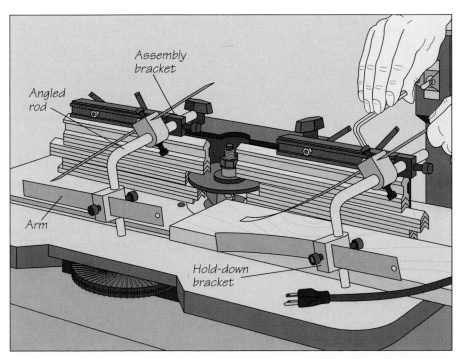

Assembly bracket

Angled rod

Arm

Hold-down bracket

2 Installing hold downs on the fence

The shaper fence should be used with hold downs or featherboards whenever possible to keep the workpiece flat against the table and fence. Install a hold-down device on your shaper fence following the manufacturer's instructions. For the spring-type model shown, attach the assembly brackets of the device to the fence brackets, then mount the angled rods on the assembly brackets. Position the metal arms of each rod so that one presses down on the workpiece and the other applies lateral pressure on the stock toward the fence. Lock the arms in place by tightening the hold-down brackets using a hex wrench *(left)*.

TWO SHAPER GUARDS AND A FENCE

The two guards shown on this page are constructed entirely from ¾-inch plywood. Easy to assemble and set up, each is designed to protect your fingers from the cutter.

The version at right is ideal for fence-guided operations. Cut the guard in the shape of an arc large enough to extend from the fence and shield the cutter completely. The support board should be wide enough to be clamped to the fence with the guard as close as possible to the cutter without touching it. Screw the guard flush with the bottom edge of the support board; countersink the fasteners. Next clamp the jig in position and mark a point on the guard above the cutter. Remove the jig and bore a 1¼-inch-diameter hole through the guard at the mark; the hole will allow you to view the cutter during shaping operations.

For freehand shaping, make a guard like the one shown below to cover the cutter from the top, back, and sides. Cut the top about 16 inches long and wide enough to extend from the back

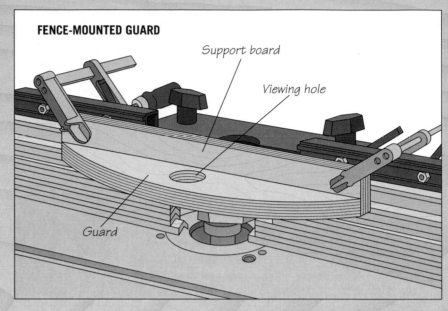

FENCE-MOUNTED GUARD

Support board

Viewing hole

Guard

of the table to about 1½ inches in front of the cutter. Miter the front ends of the sides so they can be positioned as close as possible to the cutter. Rip the sides so the top will sit above the cutter with just enough clearance for you to see the cutter. Position the top on the table and mark a point on it directly over the spindle. Cut an oval-

shaped hole through the top at your marked point; the hole should be large enough to clear the spindle and allow you to move the guard across the table slightly to accommodate different cutters. Fasten the top to the sides with countersunk screws.

To use the guard, position it on the table with the spindle projecting through the top, and with the sides as close as possible to the cutting edges. Clamp the guard in place.

The shop-made fence shown on page 127, made from ¾-inch plywood and a few scraps of lumber, is an inexpensive alternative to a commercial fence. It is also very safe, since the cutting edges only project through a narrow slot in the fence and are covered by a guard. Start by cutting the base and upright from plywood. Make both pieces as long as the table; the base should be about 12 inches wide and the upright about 3 inches wide. Before assembling the pieces, cut a notch

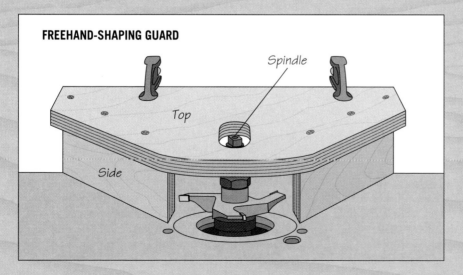

FREEHAND-SHAPING GUARD

Spindle

Top

Side

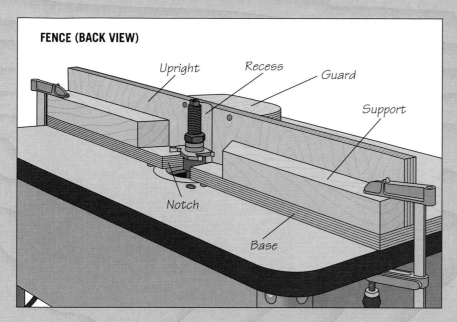

FENCE (BACK VIEW)

Upright Recess Guard Support Notch Base

Attach the supports to the base, then screw the upright to the supports; countersink your fasteners.

To set up the fence, use a saber saw to cut a precise slot for the cutter. Or, place the fence on the shaper table, clamping only one end in position. With the cutter you plan to use installed on the spindle, turn on the shaper and carefully pivot the free end of the fence into the cutter until the cutting edges rout a slot through the upright and project by the proper amount. Then turn off the machine and clamp the free end of the fence to the table. Finally, cut a plywood guard large enough to extend over the cutter and screw it to the upright, flush with the top edge.

into the back edge of the base in line with the spindle and carve a recess across the width of the upright's back face; align the recess with the notch.

Next, cut the supports from 2-by-2 stock. One end of the supports should be flush with the ends of the base; miter the other end to clear the cutter.

To make a cut, feed the workpiece into the cutter with both hands, using featherboards to apply pressure against the upright and the base of the fence.

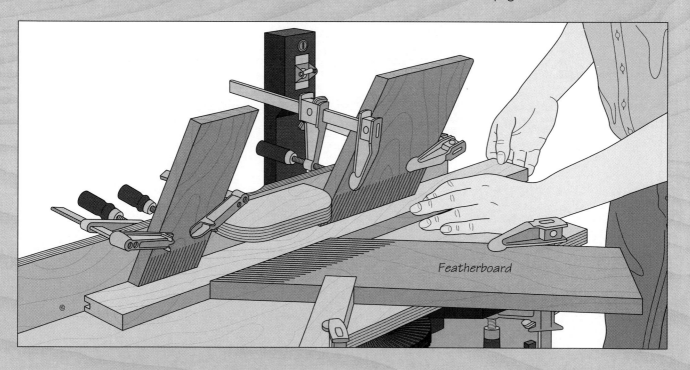

Featherboard

F ew tools can match the shaper's precision and efficiency for carving decorative contours in wood and cutting perfect joints. Shapers handle both straight and curved cuts. Straight cuts on the edges of most workpieces should always be guided by a fence. A typical setup is illustrated below. If you are shaping stock that is shorter than 12 inches, or cutting into the end or face of a board, you should use a specialty jig like the tenoner or miter gauge shown on page 129, rather than the fence.

Curved cuts can be performed freehand or using a template. Templates are simple to build and can be custom-made for the job at hand. Examples are shown on pages 130 and 131. A rub bearing should be mounted on the spindle for many straight cuts; it is a must if you are using a template. The rest of the procedure is straightforward: The workpiece

With a drawer joint cutter installed on its spindle, a shaper can make quick work of cutting both parts of a drawer joint. Featuring interlocking tongues and grooves and twice the gluing surface of a simple butt joint, the drawer joint is simple but strong.

is fastened to the template with double-sided tape or toggle clamps. The template rides on the rub bearing while the cutter shapes the workpiece. The width of cut is determined by the relative diameters of the rub bearing and the cutter.

Another option for curve-cutting is a shop-made jig. A V-block jig for circle cuts is shown on page 132.

Freehand shaping—cutting without a template or jig—can be performed only with partial cuts, in which the cutter bites into a portion of an edge while the rest rides against the rub bearing. Even these cuts are not quite "freehand"; a starting pin must be installed on the table to brace the work before it contacts the rub bearing, preventing kickback.

As you would with a router, make a few shallow passes to reach your final depth, rather than trying to remove all the waste in a single pass. For best results, use a smooth, even feed speed and cut with the grain, rather than against it. Shaping against grain can result in tearout or kickback. When you are cutting end grain, place a backup board behind the workpiece to prevent tearout.

STRAIGHT CUTS

Shaping an edge

Once the cutter and fence are set up, secure your workpiece with three featherboards. Clamp two featherboards to the fence, one on either side of the guard, and a third to the table in line with the cutter. Clamp a support board at a 90° angle to the featherboard for extra pressure. To make the cut, feed the workpiece into the cutter with both hands, as shown on page 127. Once the trailing end of the board reaches the table's edge, finish the pass using a push stick *(right)*, or by moving to the outfeed side of the table and pulling the stock past the cutter.

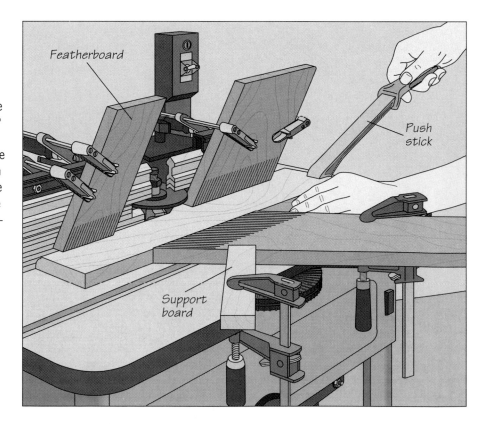

Featherboard

Push stick

Support board

CUTTING A DRAWER JOINT

1 Cutting the drawer sides

For these cuts, the shaper is fitted with a router spindle and drawer joint bit. The joint is cut in two stages. The drawer sides are cut first, held upright in a tenoning jig. The drawer front and back are then cut face down in a miter gauge. Install a commercial tenoner on the table following the manufacturer's instructions; the model shown slides in the miter slot. Clamp the workpiece to the jig, protecting the stock with a wood pad. To prevent tearout, place a backup board behind the trailing edge of the workpiece. Follow the manufacturer's directions to adjust the jig for the depth and width of cut. Feed the work smoothly into the bit *(right)*.

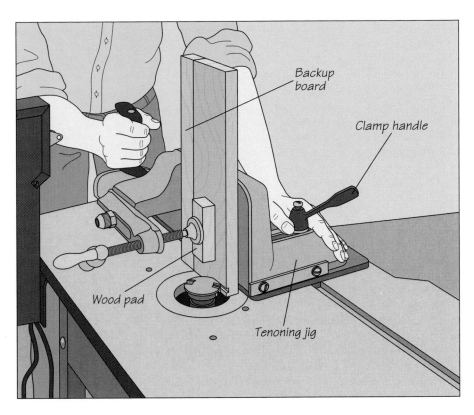

Backup board

Clamp handle

Wood pad

Tenoning jig

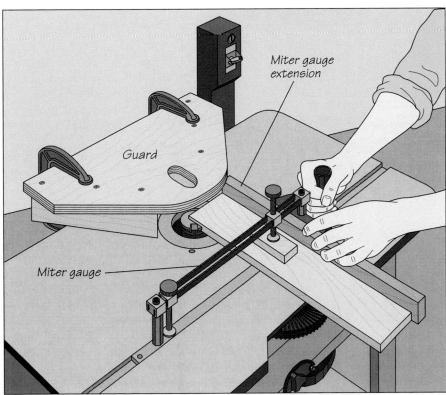

Miter gauge extension

Guard

Miter gauge

2 Cutting the drawer front and back

Remove the tenoner from the table and install a miter gauge equipped with hold downs. Also clamp a guard to the table to protect your hands from the bit; see page 126 for details on building the guard shown in this illustration. Protect the stock with a wood pad and clamp the workpiece to the miter gauge; position the board laterally on the jig for the width of cut. To provide additional support and reduce tearout, screw an extension board to the miter gauge. Slide the miter gauge and the stock as a unit into the cutter *(left)*. Test the fit of the joint and adjust the height of the bit, if necessary. If you want the drawer front to overhang the sides, as in the photo on page 128, you will need to make a few passes, increasing the width of cut slightly each time. Clamp a stop block to the extension board for repeat cuts.

PROFILING JIG

A profiling jig like the one shown at right is a timesaving device for shaping several copies of the same curved pattern. The jig features a template of the shape you wish to reproduce. Clamp your stock atop the template, which will follow a rub bearing on the spindle, enabling the cutting edge to reproduce the pattern on the workpiece.

Make the template from a piece of ¾-inch plywood that is larger than the workpiece to provide a bearing surface before and after the cut. Cut the pattern with a band saw or a saber saw, then carefully sand the edges that will ride along the rub bearing. The template must be smooth since any imperfections will be transferred to your stock. Next cut your workpieces roughly to size, oversizing the edge to be shaped by about ⅛ inch. Position the workpiece on the template, aligning the cutting mark on the edge to be shaped with the curved edge of the template. Using a pencil, outline the workpiece on the surface of the template. Fasten two guide blocks to the template from underneath with countersunk screws, lining up the edges of the blocks with the marked outline. To complete the jig, screw a toggle clamp to each guide block.

Install a rub bearing and a straight cutter on the shaper. Adjust the height of the cutter so it will shape the full width of the workpiece; the rub bearing should be the same diameter as the cutter. Secure the workpiece on the jig, making sure to butt the stock flush against the guide blocks. Set the jig on the table and

adjust the spindle height so the cutting edges will shape the entire edge of the workpiece. Also make sure the template and the rub bearing are aligned.

To make the cut, turn on the shaper with the jig and workpiece

clear of the cutter. Holding the toggle clamps, feed the workpiece into the cutter *(below)*. Apply slight pressure to press the template against the rub bearing. Keep the template in contact with the bearing throughout the operation.

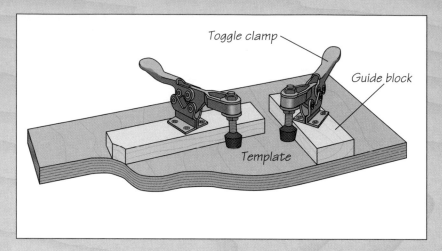

Toggle clamp

Guide block

Template

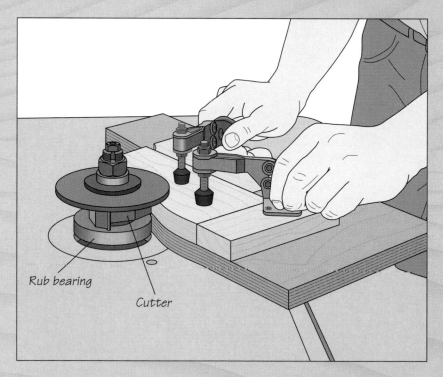

Rub bearing

Cutter

SHAPING WITH A TEMPLATE

1 Setting up and starting the cut

Build a template as you would a pro-filing jig *(page 130)*; rather than edge blocks and toggle clamps, this template has a 2-by-4 handle screwed to it from underneath. Bevel the upper edges of the block for comfort. Clamp a guard to the table to cover the cutter. Then cut the workpiece roughly to size, making it several inches larger than you need so it can be screwed to the template. Locate the screw holes in the waste section you will cut away after the shaping operation is completed. Start the cut as you would with the profiling jig, gripping the template handle with your right hand to feed the workpiece and applying lateral pressure with your left hand to keep the template flush against the rub bearing *(right)*.

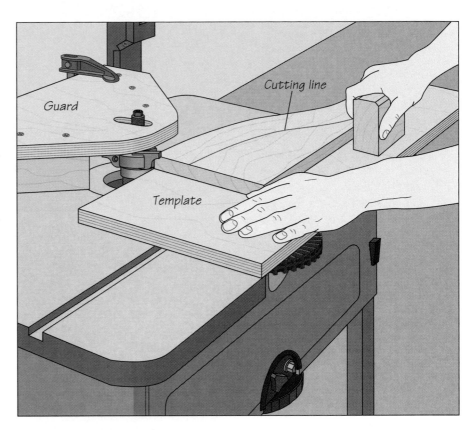

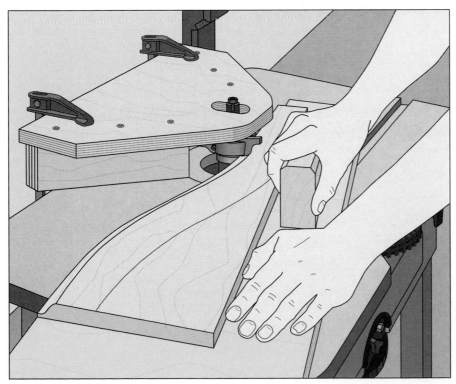

2 Completing the cut

Continue feeding with your right hand while using your left hand to keep the template in contact with the rub bearing; the template should ride along the bearing as the cutter shapes the workpiece. As the trailing end of the stock reaches the cutter, gradually slide your left hand toward the back of the workpiece *(left)*, maintaining pressure against the rub bearing until the template clears the cutter. Once you have finished the cut, unscrew the workpiece from the template and trim the waste.

A JIG FOR CIRCLE CUTS

Shaping circular work freehand on the shaper can be a risky job. One way to make the task safer and more accurate is to use a V-block jig like the one shown at right to help guide the cut; build the device from a piece of ¾-inch plywood.

For most shapers, cut the jig about 24 inches long and 14 inches wide. To customize the jig for your shaper, hold it above the table flush with the back edge and mark the location of the spindle on the surface. Cut a right-angle wedge out of the jig, locating the apex of the angle at your marked point. Then cut a circle out of the jig centered on the apex; the hole should be large enough to accommodate the largest cutter you plan to use with the jig. Rout two slots into the back edge of the jig on either side of the hole—about 5 inches long and ½ inch wide—to line up with the holes in the shaper table for the fence locking rods.

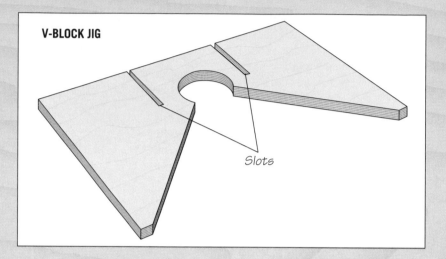

V-BLOCK JIG

Slots

Position the jig on the table, centering the bit in the hole. Seat the workpiece in the jig, butting it against both sides of the V, and adjust the jig and workpiece until the width of cut is set correctly. Tighten the fence locking handles to clamp the jig in place. You may want to make a test cut on a scrap piece to be certain that the depth and width of cut are correct.

To use the jig, turn on the shaper and butt the workpiece against the outfeed side of the V. Slowly pivot the stock into the cutter until it rests firmly in the jig's V, moving it against the direction of cutter rotation to prevent kickback *(below)*. Continue rotating the workpiece until the entire circumference has been shaped, keeping the edge in contact with both sides of the jig throughout the cut.

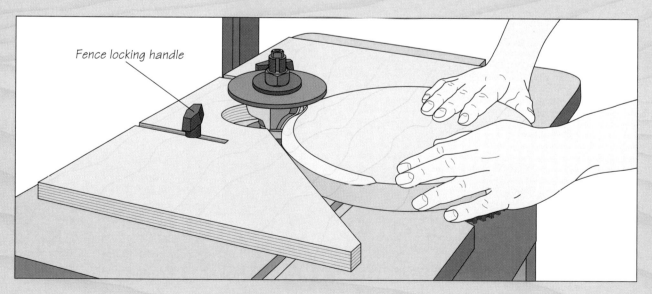

Fence locking handle

FREEHAND SHAPING

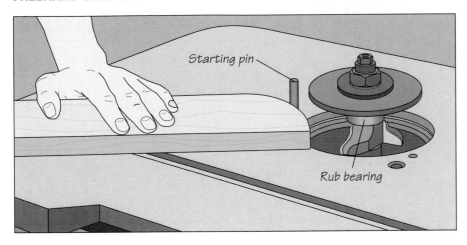

Starting pin

Rub bearing

1 Setting up the cut
Reverse the direction of cutter rotation to clockwise and place the starting pin in its hole on the infeed side of the table. This will now be the left-hand side. (For this cut, the rub bearing is mounted on the spindle above the cutter, since the bottom portion of the workpiece's edge is to be shaped.) Turn on the shaper and butt the leading end of the stock against the starting pin *(left)*.

2 Starting the cut
Bracing the workpiece against the starting pin, pivot the stock into the cutter *(right)*. As the cutter bites into the stock, it tends to kick the workpiece toward you; be sure to hold the board firmly. Once the workpiece is in contact with both the starting pin and the rub bearing, slowly swing it away from the pin while keeping it pressed against the rub bearing.

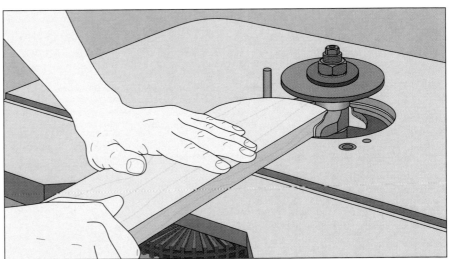

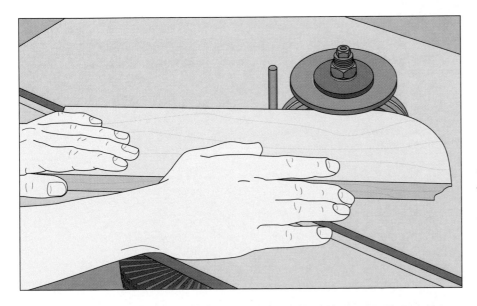

3 Completing the cut
Continue feeding the workpiece, maintaining constant pressure against the rub bearing *(left)*. Keep your hands well away from the edge of the workpiece being shaped. Once the cut is finished, slowly pull the stock away from the rub bearing and the cutter.

FRAME-AND-PANEL DOORS

Frame-and-panel construction has been popular with woodworkers for close to 500 years primarily because it offers a solution to the problem of wood movement by allowing the panel to expand and contract freely as ever-changing moisture levels in the air cause wood to swell and shrink. Humidity levels in centrally heated houses can range from 10 percent in winter to 85 percent in summer.

A frame-and-panel assembly comprises two horizontal members—rails—and two vertical stiles, all locked together with strong joints. The following pages will show you how to cut the commonly used cope-and-stick joint.

The opening in the frame is filled by a "floating" panel that sits in grooves cut in the rails and stiles. These grooves are cut on the shaper by a sticking cutter, which carves a decorative molding along

This frame-and-panel door features a sturdy frame of rails and stiles encasing a decorative floating panel. The contrast between the walnut panel and ash frame makes this door all the more striking.

the inside edges of the frame at the same time. The pieces of the frame mesh together by means of tongues and grooves cut into the ends of the rails that fit into

the grooves and molding cuts in the stiles. The rails are shaped by a coping cutter.

The panel is said to float because it is not glued in place. Instead, it fits in its grooves with room for movement. Panels are often "raised"—that is, they have bevels cut around their edges. This makes the panels easier to fit into grooves while providing decorative appeal. As shown on page 136, the shaper can also be called upon to raise panels.

A plethora of cope-and-stick cutters is manufactured specifically for frame-and-panel construction. Panel-raising bits are available in an equally diverse range. Follow the manufacturer's instructions for using these cutters.

When constructing a frame-and-panel door with the shaper, size all the components of the frame before beginning to shape. This allows you to use the same cutter setup for the entire operation.

A COPE-AND-STICK FRAME

1 Setting up for the cope cuts
Start by making the cope cuts into the ends of the rails. Install a coping cutter and ring guard on the shaper, then build a coping jig. The simple jig is made from four pieces: a ¾-inch plywood base sized to fit between the spindle and the front edge of the table, a miter bar screwed to the bottom of the base that rides in the miter slot, a 2-by-4 support board fastened atop the base flush with the back edge, and a plywood backup board screwed to the support board. To prevent tearout on the workpiece, the backup board should extend beyond the base to the desired width of cut. To complete the jig, screw two toggle clamps to the support board *(right)*. Countersink all your fasteners. To set the cutter to the correct height, mark two lines for the tongue location on the rail; the tongue should be centered between the faces of the board. Position the jig on the table and set the workpiece on the base. Adjust the cutter height to align the tongue cutter between the marks *(inset)*.

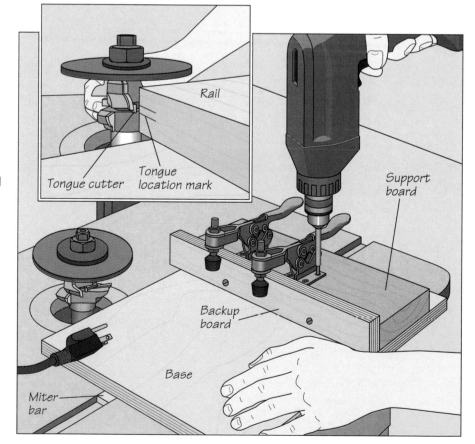

2 Making the cope cuts in the rails
Position the workpiece on the jig base flush with the end of the backup board so the cutter will shape the entire board end, then use the toggle clamps to secure the stock in place. Butt a stop block against the opposite end of the workpiece and clamp it in place. Turn on the shaper and feed the workpiece into the cutter with one hand gripping a toggle clamp and the other braced on the jig base. Remove the workpiece, turn it around in the jig and repeat the cut to shape the tongue at the other end *(right)*.

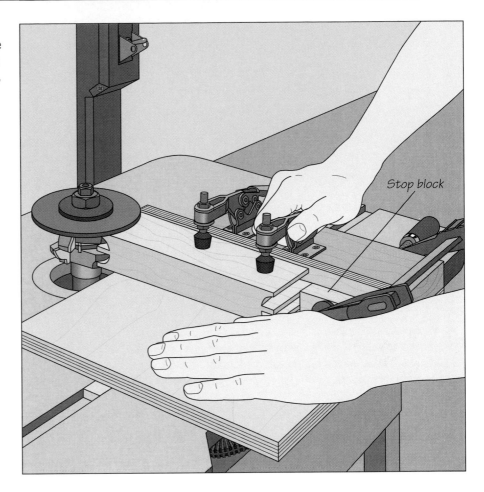

Stop block

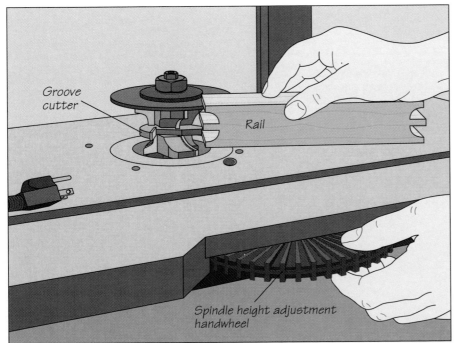

Groove cutter

Rail

Spindle height adjustment handwheel

3 Adjusting the height of the sticking bit
Once all the cope cuts are made, remove the coping cutter and install a stick cutter set on the shaper. Be sure the groove cutter is the same thickness as the tongue left by the cope cuts. This setup will shape the edges of the stiles with a decorative profile and cut grooves for the rails and the panels in one step. To set the cutting height, butt the end of one of the completed rails against the stick cutter, then adjust the height of the spindle so that the groove cutter is level with the tongue on the rail *(left)*.

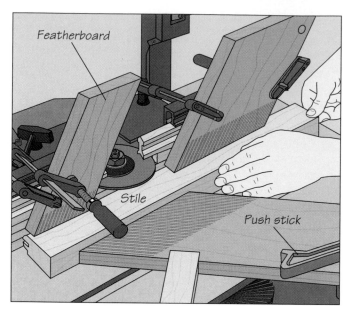

4 Making the stick cuts
For the door shown below, with straight stiles, one straight-edged rail, and one curved rail, install the fence on the table for the straight cuts. Set the cutting width for a full cut—one that will shape the entire edge of each board. To secure the stock, clamp two featherboards to the fence and one to the table (*above, left*). When feeding the workpiece into the cutter, use a push stick to complete the pass. To make the cut on the curved edge of the top rail, remove the fence and build a profiling jig based on the model shown on page 130 to guide the piece. Install a rub bearing on the spindle and adjust the height of the cutter to accommodate the thickness of the jig. Feed the rail into the cutter, holding the jig's toggle clamps firmly (*above, right*).

MAKING A RAISED PANEL

1 Cutting the panel to size
Assemble the frame dry and measure the opening between the rails and stiles. Add ½ inch to each of the dimensions to allow for the ¼ inch along the panel edges that will fit into the frame grooves (*right*). For the curved top edge of the panel, outline the profile of the curved rail on the stock, then draw a parallel line offset from the first by ¼ inch. (The dotted lines in the illustration represent the actual edges of the panel; the solid lines represent the frame opening.) Make the straight cuts to size the panel on the table saw, ripping first, then crosscutting. Cut the curved top of the panel on the band saw.

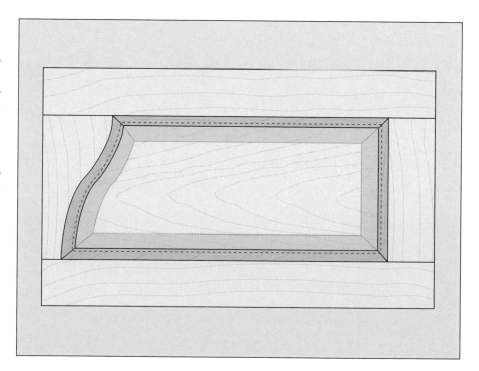

2 Setting up a panel-raising jig

Build a jig to guide the panel into the cutter safely and accurately. The jig consists of a template of ¾-inch plywood, cut to the same length as the panel, but about 12 inches wider to accommodate edge blocks; reproduce the curve of the panel's edge on the template. Center the panel on the template, then butt edge blocks against the panel and screw them to the template; to reduce tearout, the blocks should extend to the end of the template on the outfeed side of each cut. Screw a toggle clamp onto each edge block and secure the panel to the jig, making sure its ends are flush with the template ends *(right)*. (You may wish to make a test cut on a scrap piece, test its fit in the panel and adjust the cutter height, if necessary.)

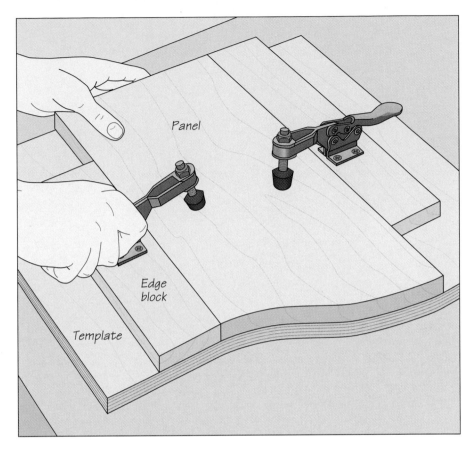

3 Raising the panel ends

Install a rub bearing and a panel-raising cutter on the shaper spindle. Adjust the cutting height to make a partial cut. (Do not attempt to raise the panel ends with one cut. You will need to make two or more passes, test-fitting after each cut until the panel fits properly into the rails.) Clamp a guard to the table to protect your hands from the cutter. Turn on the shaper, butt the template against the rub bearing, and feed the curved edge of the panel into the cutter, holding the jig firmly with both hands. Turn the jig around and repeat the procedure to raise the other end of the panel. Make successive passes, lowering the cutter until the panel fits in its mating groove *(left)*.

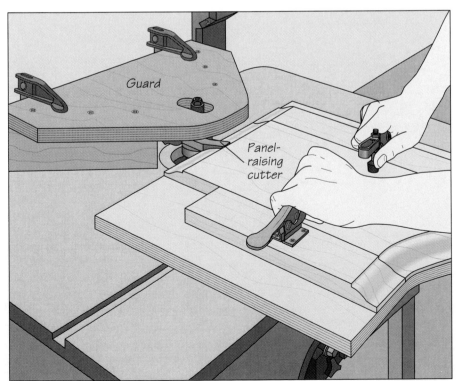

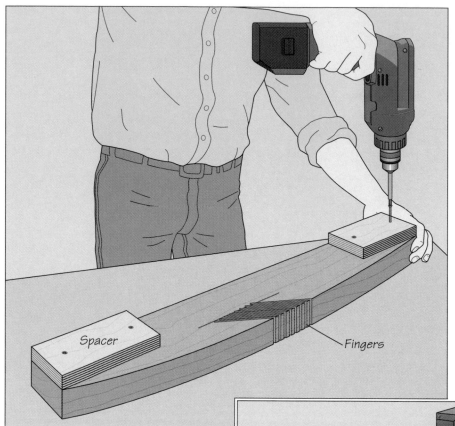

4 **Making a featherboard for the straight cuts**

To raise the sides of the panel safely, build an extra-wide featherboard. It will not only press the panel against the table, but also shield your fingers from the cutter. Cut a 2-by-4 to the length of your fence. Set the board against the fence and use a pencil to outline the location of the cutter on it. Then use the band saw to cut a series of ¼-inch-wide slots at a 30° to 45° angle within the outline, creating a row of sturdy but pliable fingers. Also curve the bottom edge of the featherboard so that only the fingers contact the panel during the shaping operation. Screw two spacers to the back face of the featherboard to enable the jig to clear the cutter; countersink the fasteners *(left)*.

Spacer

Fingers

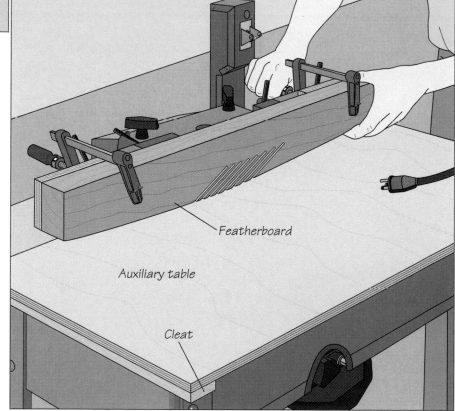

5 **Setting up the shaper for straight cuts**

To avoid having to adjust the spindle height for shaping the panel sides, install an auxiliary plywood table on the shaper that is the same thickness as the profiling jig template you used to raise the ends *(page 137)*. Attach a cleat to each end of the plywood piece to hold it snugly in place. Clamp the featherboard to the fence *(right)* so it will apply pressure on the panel as you make the pass. Advance the fence and featherboard away from the rub bearing on the first pass so you remove only a portion of the waste.

Featherboard

Auxiliary table

Cleat

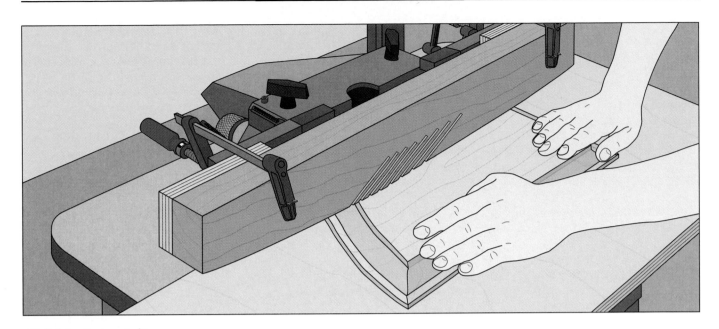

6 Raising the panel sides

Turn on the shaper and use your right hand to slowly feed the workpiece into the cutter; use your left hand to keep the panel against the fence. Turn the panel around and repeat the cut to shape the other side of the panel *(above)*. Move the fence closer to the rub bearing and shape both sides of the panel again. Make as many passes as necessary—two or three are usually sufficient—until the fence and rub bearing are aligned; this final pass will give you the full width and depth of cut.

ASSEMBLING THE DOOR

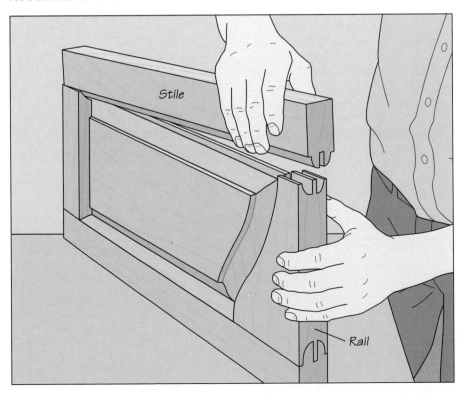

Stile

Rail

Test assembling and gluing up the pieces
Join a rail and a stile, then seat the panel between them. Set the stile on a work surface and add the second rail and stile *(left)*. Mark all the joints with a pencil to help you assemble the pieces when you apply the glue in the final assembly. The panel should fit snugly but easily. If it is too tight, make another light pass on the shaper along the ill-fitting edge or end. Assemble the door again. Once you are satisfied with the fit, apply glue to all the contacting surfaces of the frame. Do not spread any adhesive in the panel grooves; the panel must be free to move within the frame. Glue up the door, securing it with bar clamps.

GLOSSARY

A-B-C

Arbor: A motor-driven shaft that turns rotating blades or other cutting implements.

Bead: A rounded, convex shape cut in wood, usually along an edge.

Bevel cut: A cut at an angle from face to face through the thickness or along the length of a workpiece.

Box joint: Identical interlocking fingers that mesh to form a corner joint.

Butterfly key joint: A joint featuring a double-wing-shaped hardwood key glued into a recess to strengthen a board or glued-up panel.

Carcase: The box-like body of a piece of furniture.

Centering pin: A machined aluminum pin inserted in a router collet and used with a dial indicator or feeler gauge to check collet runout.

Chamfer: A bevel cut along the edge of a workpiece.

Collet: The sleeve that grips the shank of a router bit.

Cope-and-stick joint: A method of joining stiles and rails in frame-and-panel construction. Tongues in the rails mesh with grooves in the stiles; a decorative molding is cut along the inside edge of the frame.

Coping bit: A router bit that cuts both a decorative molding and tongue in a workpiece, allowing the stock to be joined to a board with a matching groove.

Countersink: Drilling a hole that allows a screw head to lie flush with or slightly below the surface of a workpiece.

Cove: A rounded, concave decorative profile cut in wood, usually along an edge.

D-E-F-G-H

Dado: A rectangular channel cut across the grain of a workpiece.

Edge guide: A straightedge that guides a tool during a cut.

Edge jointing: Cutting thin shavings from the edge of a workpiece until it is flat and square to the face.

Featherboard: A piece of wood with thin fingers or "feathers" along one end to hold a workpiece securely against the fence or table of a power tool.

Fence: An adjustable guide to keep the edge of a workpiece a set distance from the cutting edge of a tool.

Glue joint: An interlocking tongue and groove commonly used to join boards edge-to-edge.

Groove: A cut along the grain of a workpiece, forming a rectangular channel; frequently decorative, but may form part of joint.

Half-blind dovetail: Similar to a through dovetail joint, except that the pins are not cut through the entire thickness of the workpiece in order to conceal the end grain of the tail boards.

Hanger bolt: A bolt with no head; one end of the bolt has wood screw threads while the other end features machine threads to accept a nut.

I-J-K-L-M-N

Infeed: The direction from which a workpiece is fed into the blade or bit of a power tool.

Jig: A device for guiding a tool or holding a workpiece in position.

Kickback: The tendency of a workpiece to be thrown back toward the operator of a power tool.

Laminate: A thin layer of material, such as veneer or plastic, used to cover core stock.

Marquetry: Decorative inlays of veneers, metals, or other materials.

Miter-and-spline joint: A joint featuring two mitered or beveled surfaces butted together and reinforced with a spline.

Miter gauge: A device that slides in a slot on a saw, shaper, or router table, providing support for the stock as it moves past the blade or bit; can be adjusted to different angles.

Molding cutter head: A solid-metal wheel that accepts a set of three identical cutter knives, enabling a table saw or radial arm saw to cut molding.

Mortise: A rectangular or oval hole cut into a piece of wood to accept a mating tenon.

Mortise-and-tenon joint: A joinery technique in which a projecting tenon on one board fits into a mortise in another.

O-P-Q-R

Ogee: A decorative molding with an S-shaped profile.

Outfeed: The side of a power tool blade or bit to which a workpiece exits after cutting.

Pilot bearing: A cylindrical metal collar either above or below the router bit's cutting edge that rides along the workpiece or a template, guiding the bit during a cut.

Pin router: A table assembly that suspends the router above the workpiece; a fence or guide pin on the table guides the workpiece into the bit.

Plunge router: A router whose entire motor assembly is mounted above the base of the tool on spring-loaded columns; downward pressure on the handles feeds the bit into the wood.

Push block or push stick: A device used to feed a workpiece into the blade or cutter of a tool to protect the operator's fingers.

Rabbet: A step-like cut in the edge or end of a board; usually forms part of a joint.

Rail: A board that runs along the underside of a tabletop to which the legs of the table are attached; also, the horizontal member of a frame-and-panel assembly.

Raised panel: A piece of wood that forms the center of a frame-and-panel assembly. Beveling the edges of the panel "raises" the middle portion.

Rub bearing: A ball-bearing collar mounted on a shaper spindle either above or below the cutter to provide a bearing surface for a workpiece or template.

Rule joint: A joinery method commonly used in drop-leaf tables; the tabletop has a convex profile, the leaf has a matching concave cut; the two are held together by a drop-leaf hinge.

Runout: The amount of wobble that a shaper spindle or router collet imparts to a cutter when the tool is operating; 0.005 inch or less is acceptable.

S-T

Sliding dovetail joint: Similar to a tongue-and-groove joint, except the slide is shaped like the pin of a dovetail joint and the groove features a tail-like profile.

Spindle: The threaded arbor on a shaper that holds cutters and accessories.

Spline: A thin piece of wood that fits in mating grooves cut in two workpieces, reinforcing the joint between them.

Sticking bit: A router bit that cuts a decorative molding and a groove at the end or edge of a workpiece, allowing the stock to be joined to a board with a matching tongue.

Stile: The vertical member of a frame-and-panel assembly.

Stopped groove: A groove that does not run the full length or width of a workpiece.

Tearout: The tendency of a blade or cutter to tear wood fibers.

Template: A pattern used with a template guide and non-piloted router bit or a piloted bit to reproduce copies of the pattern.

Template guide: A metal collar screwed onto a router's base plate to guide a non-piloted bit during a pattern routing operation.

Tenon: A protrusion from the end of a workpiece that fits into a mortise.

Through dovetail joint: A method of joining wood by means of interlocking pins and tails; the name derives from the distinctive shape cut into the ends of the joining boards.

Tongue-and-groove: A joinery method featuring a protrusion from the edge or end of one board that fits into the groove of another.

U-V-W-X-Y-Z

Veneer: A thin layer of decorative wood laid into or over a more common wood.

INDEX

ACKNOWLEDGMENTS

The editors wish to thank the following:

ROUTER BASICS
Adjustable Clamp Co., Chicago, IL; Black & Decker/Elu Power Tools, Towson, MD; Delta International Machinery/Porter Cable, Guelph, Ont.; Freud Westmore Tools, Ltd., Mississauga, Ont.; Hitachi Power Tools U.S.A. Ltd., Norcross, GA; Lee Valley Tools Ltd., Ottawa, Ont.; Linemaster Switch Corp., Woodstock, CT; Newman Tools Inc., Montreal, Que.; Sears, Roebuck and Co., Chicago, IL; Shopsmith, Inc., Montreal, Que.; Vermont American Corp., Lincolnton, NC and Louisville, KY

EDGE FORMING
Adjustable Clamp Co., Chicago, IL; Black & Decker/Elu Power Tools, Towson, MD; Delta International Machinery/Porter Cable, Guelph, Ont.; Freud Westmore Tools, Ltd., Mississauga, Ont.; G & W Tool, Inc., Tulsa, OK; General Tools Manufacturing Co., Inc., New York, NY; Lee Valley Tools Ltd., Ottawa, Ont.; Makita Canada, Inc., Whitby, Ont.; Richards Engineering Co., Ltd., Vancouver, B.C.; Robert Larson Company, Inc., San Francisco, CA; Sandvik Saws and Tools Co., Scranton, PA; Sears, Roebuck and Co., Chicago, IL; Shopsmith, Inc., Dayton, OH and Montreal, Que.; Vermont American Corp., Lincolnton, NC and Louisville, KY

GROOVING
Adjustable Clamp Co., Chicago, IL; Black & Decker/Elu Power Tools, Towson, MD; Delta International Machinery/Porter Cable, Guelph, Ont.; Freud Westmore Tools, Ltd., Mississauga, Ont.; General Tools Manufacturing Co., Inc., New York, NY; Griset Industries, Inc., Santa Ana, CA; Hitachi Power Tools U.S.A. Ltd., Norcross, GA; Lee Valley Tools Ltd., Ottawa, Ont.; Sears, Roebuck and Co., Chicago, IL; Shopsmith Inc, Dayton, OH

ROUTER JOINERY
Adjustable Clamp Co., Chicago, IL; Black & Decker/Elu Power Tools, Towson, MD; Delta International Machinery/Porter Cable, Guelph, Ont.; Freud Westmore Tools, Ltd., Mississauga, Ont.; Hitachi Power Tools U.S.A. Ltd., Norcross, GA; Leichtung Workshops, Cleveland, OH; Leigh Industries Ltd., Port Coquitlam, B.C.; Makita Canada Ltd., Whitby, Ont.; Robert Larson Company, Inc., San Francisco, CA; Shopsmith Inc., Montreal, Que.; Vermont American Corp., Lincolnton, NC and Louisville, KY

SHAPER
Adjustable Clamp Co., Chicago, IL; Delta International Machinery/Porter Cable, Guelph, Ont.; Laguna Tools, Laguna Beach, CA; Lee Valley Tools Ltd., Ottawa, Ont.; Newman Tools Inc., Montreal, Que.; Richards Engineering Co., Ltd., Vancouver, B.C.; Sears, Roebuck and Co., Chicago, IL; Shopsmith, Inc., Montreal, Que.

The following persons also assisted in the preparation of this book:

Réjean Coté, Lorraine Doré, Réjean Garand, Graphor Consultation, Irene Huang, Claude Martel, Geneviève Monette, Tamiko Watanabe

PICTURE CREDITS

Cover Robert Chartier
6, 7 Glen Hartjes/Image Studios
8, 9 Ian Gittler
10, 11 Ian Gittler
37 Courtesy Williams & Hussey Machine Co.
91 Courtesy Jointmaker/Vega Enterprises
117 Courtesy Reliable Cutting Tools
119 Courtesy Scars, Roebuck and Co.